1.00

JEAN du SABLE
Father of Chicago

Also by the same author:

The Magnificent Bastards
Mission Incredible
Battle of the Bismarck Sea
Jim Beckwourth: Explorer-Patriot of the Rockies

Lawrence Cortesi

JEAN du SABLE
Father of Chicago

CHILTON BOOK COMPANY
Philadelphia · New York

Copyright © 1972 by Lawrence J. Cortesi
First Edition
All Rights Reserved

Published in Philadelphia by Chilton Book Company
and simultaneously in Ontario, Canada,
by Thomas Nelson & Sons, Ltd.

Library of Congress Cataloging in Publication Data

Cortesi, Lawrence.
    Jean duSable: father of Chicago.

    SUMMARY: A biography of the black Haitian who
was the first non-Indian to settle and establish a trading community on the site of present-day Chicago.
    Bibliography: p.
    1. Pointe du Sable, Jean Baptiste, 1745?–1818—
Juvenile literature.   2.   Chicago—History—To   1875
—Juvenile literature.   [1. Pointe du Sable, Jean Baptiste,   1745?–1818.   2.   Chicago—History—To   1875.
3. Negroes—Biography.] I. Title.
F548.4.P742   977.3'11'020924   [B]   72-3791
ISBN 0-8019-5678-1

Designed by Cypher Associates
Manufactured in the United States of America

To Milo Milton Quaife
Historian Emeritus, Detroit Public Library
who did so much to enlighten history
about Jean duSable

JEAN du SABLE

Father of Chicago

Foreword

The city of Chicago, Illinois, has a Kinzie Park, Kinzie Bridge, Kinzie Street, and Kinzie Building, a name honoring John C. Kinzie, early nineteenth-century trader and merchant as the father of Chicago. The honor is a hundred-and-fifty-year myth.

True, Kinzie did operate a trading post there in the early 1800's when the United States government built Fort Dearborn on the east bank of the Chicago River. Historical records from the old fort gave the following price list for goods from John Kinzie's trading post:

Tobacco/50¢ a pound
Powder/$1.00 a pound
Shot/25¢ a pound
Potatoes/60¢ a bushel
Corn/$1.50 and $2.50 a bushel
Butter/50¢ a pound
Whiskey/$1.25 a gallon

American homesteaders from the East trekking westward over the flat plains that later became Chicago found every-

1

thing from stables to lodging houses under the control of Kinzie, as did Indian, French Canadian and American fur trappers.

A civil engineer named James Thompson on August 4, 1830, filed the township plan giving Chicago its first legal geographical location. At the dedication ceremonies he praised the "Father of Chicago," John Kinzie. A few years later Juliette Augusta Kinzie, daughter-in-law of John, strengthened the Kinzie myth when she published *Wau Bun —The Early Days of the Continent* in which she told how her father-in-law journeyed from Virginia to the Great Lakes at the turn of the nineteenth century to establish his trading post on the St. Joseph River in Michigan among the Potawatomi Indians, and developed early Chicago on the shores of Lake Michigan where, in the Massacre of 1813, he saved many of the civilians.

Late nineteenth-century writers like John Caton and John Wentworth, members of the Caxton Club, an early Chicago historical society, in such books as *The Story of Chicago* and the *Fall of the Illinois* used the *Wau Bun* book and Fort Dearborn records to promote John Kinzie as the father of Chicago. On November 10, 1868, the elderly and respected Augusta Kinzie, speaking at the fiftieth anniversary celebration of the birth of Chicago, thanked all who were honoring her father-in-law. Subsequently, historians merely picked through the reams of information penned earlier, so that by the turn of the twentieth century history had firmly established John Kinzie as the father of Chicago.

Most peculiar was the void in Chicago's history between 1675 and 1800. Not a single member of the Caxton Club or the later Fergus Series historians wrote a paragraph on Chicago between the time of LaSalle in 1675 until the advent of John Kinzie in 1800. It was as though the Lake Michigan plain that later became Chicago did not exist for this one-and-a-quarter century. Fortunately, early 1900 historians like Milo Milton Quaife, Bessie Louise Pierce and Harry Hansen, wondering, probed into Chicago's history between 1700 and 1800, dug out the truth and proved that the Caxton Club and

Fergus Club writers had enshrined a Johnny-come-lately as Chicago's founder.

Buried under the overwhelming histories and monuments dedicated to John C. Kinzie they found their first clue in a corroded plaque on an old dilapidated building, the Kirk Soap Factory, at the corner of Pine and (ironically) Kinzie Streets. On its crumbling walls hung a faded, neglected plaque that read:

On this site, in 1772, Jean Baptiste Pointe duSable, a Negro from Santo Domingo, built the first cabin at Chicago.

If the plaque were accurate then this Negro from Santo Domingo had settled at Chicago nearly thirty years ahead of the "Father of Chicago." The first confirmation of its accuracy was discovered in *Wau Bun* itself. Augusta Kinzie had written there:

Jean Baptiste Pointe duSable left Chicago in 1800 to settle at Peoria and live with an old friend, Clemorgan, another Negro (sic) from Santo Domingo.

The reference to Jacques Clemorgan, a West Indies neighbor and close friend of Jean duSable, was to a white man who left his own mark on the Midwest. Mrs. Kinzie in her book also admits that her father-in-law first purchased Chicago properties in 1803—certain commercial buildings (trading post, barns, etc.)—from one Jean LeLime. Historical records show that earlier Jean duSable, as owner and manager of a successful trading post at Chicago, *employed* Jean Le-Lime, so he was established long before Kinzie or LeLime.

Archives in Canada revealed too that Colonel Arent Schuyler de Peyster, commanding the English outpost of Fort Michelmackinac on Lake Huron during the Revolutionary War, wrote to British general Sir Henry Clinton in 1778:

Jean Baptiste Pointe duSable is a handsome Negro, well educated and settled in trade at Eschikagou (the original Indian name for Chicago). *However, he is much in the French interest.*

(De Peyster worried about duSable's French interests because France had joined the American cause in 1778.)

Next, an old ledger of Detroit merchant Thomas Smith's indicated that he dealt with Jean duSable at Eschikagou from December 25, 1773 to April 16, 1783. James May, another eighteenth-century merchant from Detroit, also attempted to establish a trade with Jean duSable when in 1790 he sent his clerk, Hugh Howard, to St. Louis on business asking that he stop at Eschikagou to determine if they could sell wholesale goods to this Negro trader. Howard arrived at Eschikagou on May 10, 1790 and wrote in his journal:

At the des Plains (sic) [the French name for the site of present-day Chicago] *we found the trading post well stocked. We exchanged our canoe for a pirogue* [a large French canoe] *to continue our journey down the Mississippi River. We also obtained considerable bread, flour, and pork.*

The Indians themselves refute the John Kinzie claim to Father of Chicago. The Potawatomi tribe lived on the Eschikagou plain. Old Chief Black Partridge, who told stories to the children around the Kinzie mansion in the early 1800's stated: "The first white man to settle at Eschikagou was a black man, a quite black Frenchman named Jean Baptiste Pointe du Sable." And when the Potawatomis burned Fort Dearborn and Chicago in 1813, surprisingly they spared several buildings, all former properties of Jean Baptiste Pointe duSable, in recognition of their long friendship with him.

The bill of sale dated May 17, 1800, offered the final and most important proof. The document showed that the French Negro sold out his interests in Chicago in 1800 to his employee, Jean LeLime, for six thousand livres (the French monetary system for North America), who in turn sold these properties to John Kinzie three years later. The bill of sale indexed the following Baptiste properties at Eschikagou:

On the river bank a mansion house that included four glass doors, eleven copper kettles, and a French cabinet of walnut.

A long low building (trading post) with a piazza along the front of it, 24' by 40', ranging in depth to four or five rooms.

4

Two barns 24′ by 30′ and 28′ by 40′.

A bakehouse 18′ by 20′.

Several outhouses, a poultry house, a smoke house, blacksmith shop, and cut lumber for a third stable.

Eight axes, seven saws, seven scythes, eight sickles, three carts, one plow, a ring saw, and a cross cut saw with 7″ blade.

Livestock: two mules, two calves, two oxen, thirty head of cattle, thirty hogs, and forty-four hens.

The most remarkable item in this document of May 17, 1800, was the witness to this bill of sale between Jean duSable and Jean LeLime: None other than *John Kinzie*, the "Father of Chicago." (This bill of sale document is still on file at the Wayne County Document Building in Detroit, Michigan, where historian Milo Milton Quaife first discovered it in 1913.)

There is every reason to suspect that Jean LeLime was a mere front man for John Kinzie who had apparently learned of the proposed construction of Fort Dearborn and prevailed upon Jean LeLime to buy the duSable properties for him since Jean duSable did not trust him. Thus, in 1803, when the United States came to Chicago to build the fort John Kinzie was there ready to serve them in trade, and by the time Americans came in large numbers after the establishment of Fort Dearborn John Kinzie was in charge of everything from trading post to stables. Pioneers crossing the Eschikagou plains on their way to western homesteads bought from Kinzie and used the Kinzie portage across the plains. So began the myth of John Kinzie as the Father of Chicago.

From the very first years of North American exploration in the 16th century the Eschikagou plain was regarded as a strategic portage on the great inland water route between the Atlantic Ocean and the Gulf of Mexico. One need only examine the importance of present-day Chicago to verify this fact. However, the area had been a centuries-old battleground among hostile warring Indians who welcomed neither each other nor outsiders, so none of the early French explorers could establish a settlement on this Lake Michigan plain.

As early as 1534 the Indians told French explorer Jacques Cartier about the Eschikagou portage that led to the Mississippi River, the Father of Waters. Cartier sailed westward through the St. Lawrence River but never advanced beyond Lake Ontario in his quest for a northwest passage to the Pacific Ocean. In 1608 Samuel de Champlain, who founded the first permanent French settlement in Quebec, also explored the wilderness to the west but reached only the Great Lakes. In 1635 Jean Nicolet became the first non-Indian to set foot on the Eschikagou portage. He crossed it but stopped at the Illinois River because of continual Indian attacks, returning to Quebec convinced that the Indians in this area would destroy any settlement on des Plaines portage.

Not until 1673 did another Frenchman come to Eschikagou. When Louis Joliet saw the marvelous plain that bordered Lake Michigan he built a rude cabin there as a base to explore the Father of Waters beyond the Illinois River, but within three weeks hostile Indians drove him back to Quebec.

Only a few months later, in September, 1673, the French missionary explorer, Father Jacques Marquette, came to Eschikagou. He tried to Christianize the savage Indians who constantly clashed with one another on the Eschikagou battleground. He explained his disappointment in his diary:

The des Plains (sic) portage (Eschikagou) offers a fine means of communication between the Great Lakes and the Mississippi River. But, unless something can be done about the Indians it will be impossible to build a settlement here.

Finally, the great explorer, the Sierre de LaSalle, charted the entire length of the Mississippi River to the Gulf of Mexico. He proved beyond question that the Eschikagou portage connected a wondrous two-thousand-mile water route through the heart of the continent between the Atlantic

Ocean and the Gulf of Mexico. A settlement at Eschikagou could link the vast French territories of Quebec to the Mississippi River. In fact, LaSalle believed that such a settlement at Eschikagou could develop into a city as important as Quebec or Montreal. He built Fort Crevecour on the southern part of the Eschikagou plain for protection against the Indians. But while LaSalle returned to Quebec for more supplies the Indians drove off the men who had remained at the fort and burned it down.

The English were even less successful because of hostile Ottawa and Miami tribes, the great English explorer, Sir William Johnson, being able to penetrate no further than the Ohio valley.

For nearly two centuries the Eschikagou plain had been off limits to white men because of the never ending feuds among Ottawa, Miami, and Illinois tribes. From Quebec, the French could settle no closer to Eschikagou than Detroit; from New Orleans come no further north than Kaskaskia, a settlement just below the Illinois River. The English had fared even worse, having barely penetrated the Appalachian Mountains. The English, French, and later the Spanish were forced to follow the Ohio River valley to travel from the Mississippi River to the eastern coast of North America.

Jean Baptiste Pointe duSable, a native of Haiti in the Caribbean, was born a free man even though black. He enjoyed no titles of rank or nobility in the French aristocracy; he was no explorer, held no high place in the French government, had no influence at the Paris court and no legions of armed men. Yet Pointe duSable broke the two centuries of failure and started a settlement and trading post on the Eschikagou plain.

Eschikagou was already a thriving community by the time of the Revolutionary War. The English and Americans, as well as the French and Spanish, regarded Eschikagou as the key to the west. Both the English Colonel Arent de Peyster and the American Colonel George Rogers Clark courted the French Negro. Also, despite the fact that most of the English forts in the Midwest had come under American control by 1800, the new United States government chose to build Fort Dearborn at Eschikagou, recognizing its location as strategic for westbound homesteaders when the Great Lakes area was opened to settlement.

Who was Jean Baptiste Pointe duSable, the "Negro from Santo Domingo (who) built the first cabin at Chicago in 1772"? Why did he come to the Eschikagou plain in the first place? And how did Jean duSable change this Indian battle-ground to a continental crossroads when men more powerful than he had met only with failure for the previous two centuries?

A wealth of material has now emerged on Jean duSable and his life in Eschikagou. Many historians still differ on his earlier background. The Nathan Matson papers in the Wisconsin Historical Collection appear to be the most reliable, since Matson obtained his information on Jean duSable's early life from duSable's own grandson.

Chapter One

Jean Baptiste Pointe duSable was born in San Marc, Haiti, in 1745. Although a Negro, neither he nor his parents suffered hardship because of race for, unlike the Spanish or Portuguese, the French had not enslaved all blacks. Their colony in Haiti contained many free Negroes who enjoyed the same freedoms and privileges as other French subjects. In fact, France had in 1685 passed the *Code Noir* (Code for blacks) that insisted on humane treatment for all Negroes, including slaves.

At any rate, Jean duSable was a free Negro. His father had been a mate aboard a French privateer that preyed on Spanish merchant ships in the Caribbean, attacks which often triggered retaliation. In 1755 three Spanish men-of-war sailed into San Marc harbor, loosed a heavy bombardment on the port town, and followed up the cannonade by landing troops. The ravaging invaders burned, looted, and killed without mercy.

Among the victims of the Spanish assault were the duSables. The Spaniards burned their home to the ground and killed Jean's beautiful mother, Suzanne, when she resisted their advances. They also planned to make off with as many Negroes as possible to sell as slaves. When the terrified ten-year-old Jean duSable kicked and struggled to avoid capture, the cruel Spaniards knocked him to the ground. One looked at him with a derisive sneer:

"Don't you know you're black? You're only good for slavery."

Jean never forgot the invaders' cruelty. He would hate the Spaniards for the rest of his life. He would hate even more man's injustice to man.

Fortunately a French fleet, warned earlier of the attack on their Haitian port, arrived at San Marc and routed the Spaniards before they could make off with any prisoners. Jean's father was overcome by grief when he learned what had happened. Now with a motherless ten-year-old son he gave up the sea, and with the money earned from his maritime life bought land and started a coffee and hardwood plantation that soon prospered.

A white family named Clemorgan owned the plantation next to the duSables. One of their young sons, Jacques, grew up as a close friend of Jean. The two boys played, fished and swam in the warm Caribbean, sailed for pleasure on the blue waters and attended the St. Thomas Catholic School, always together. Their fathers also became close friends, often helping each other on their respective plantations. By the time Jean and Jacques had grown to be young men they were as close as brothers.

The boys worked hard on the plantation, reaping coffee beans, felling hardwood timber and tilling the soil. They grew to six feet, developing sinewy muscles on every part of their agile bodies, and because their fathers furnished tutors for them to advance their education beyond the St. Thomas School their mental stature kept pace with the physical. Both Jean and Jacques became skilled in mathematics, the sciences and the arts, before long they outgrew the simple life on the island. They found less and less to challenge them in Haiti. In

1763, when Jean turned nineteen years and Jacques twenty-one, their fathers summoned them to the parlor of the duSable home. Jean's father did the talking.

"Jacques," Mr. duSable said to the white boy, "your father and I have spent many days thinking about your future and Jean's. You're both strong enough to care for yourselves and intelligent enough to avoid trickery by dishonest people."

The boys merely listened.

"We have felt troubled for some time because the two of you seem unhappy," he continued. "You are grown men now, the fantasies of childhood no longer appeal to you, so perhaps you need a new life, a new outlook, a chance to develop your own independence and initiative. There is only one place you can do this," he pointed through the north window. "New France. In New France lies the future of the new world, not here on this crowded island of Haiti."

Jacques Clemorgan and Jean duSable looked at each other, but still they said nothing.

"Jacques," Jean's father said, "neither your father nor I want you to leave us. But you must live your own lives as we have lived ours. We've fitted a sloop and loaded the vessel with coffee and hardwoods. Since you are both capable navigators, I'm sure you can steer the sloop to New Orleans. There, you can sell the cargo and even the vessel itself. You'll have enough money to start any endeavor you please."

"But what shall we do, Pa-pa?" Jean asked.

"That we leave to you," Jacques' father finally spoke.

So, on a spring morning in 1764, Jean duSable and Jacques Clemorgan sailed out of San Marc, Haiti, on the sloop *Suzanne,* named after Jean's mother. Three hired crew members sailed with them. Their course was set for New Orleans across the Gulf of Mexico.

Chapter Two

Jean duSable and Jacques Clemorgan, aboard the heavily loaded *Suzanne,* wondered about their futures as they sailed across the deep blue Gulf of Mexico. They would have considerable money when they sold the rich cargo in the holds. Should they become merchants? Open an inn or cafe? Perhaps buy one or two more sloops and become shipping magnates?

Neither of them foresaw disaster. But when *Suzanne* was within a day's reach of New Orleans gray low-hanging clouds raced across the sky, darkening the horizon, and brisk winds suddenly whipped up the ocean. Rain fell. The rain grew heavier, the swells became mountainous crests and finally the winds rose to one hundred miles per hour. *Suzanne* was trapped in a hurricane!

Jean lowered sail and tightened lines, but the little sloop rolled and pitched in the heavy maelstrom. *Suzanne,* top heavy from the large cargo, could not keel herself in the rough waters. Huge waves reached out of the sea and slapped the hull like angry giants. Then, suddenly, violently, one of them smacked her and *Suzanne* flopped over on her side, washing the sloop's five passengers into the sea.

Jean duSable, who swam as well as any fish, buoyed himself on the water and scanned the boiling sea. He watched the upended *Suzanne* bounce away like a piece of floating driftwood, saw none of *Suzanne's* three crewmen but did see Jacques' grimacing face bobbing in and out of the water as he struggled to stay afloat. Jean quickly swam to Jacques, gripped him in a neck lock and then kicked toward a faintly outlined shoreline in the distance.

"S-save yourself, Jean, s-save yourself," Jacques Clemorgan gasped. "You c-can never make it with me."

Jean duSable ignored him and stroked against the battering waves and driving rain. For two hours he fought the hurricane. Finally he reached a beach, dragged his partner to solid ground, and collapsed, totally spent. The exerting swim had numbed every muscle in his body. He could barely breathe.

Clemorgan had suffered a broken leg from a piece of falling debris when *Suzanne* capsized. He could do little for his exhausted friend except crawl painfully over to spread his wet coat upon the half-conscious Jean.

By morning the Gulf of Mexico had calmed. A bright morning sun radiated a comfortable drying warmth on the two shipwrecked men. Jean had regained his strength after a full twelve hours sleep and now sought a piece of wood to make a splint for Jacques' leg. He found nothing; nor any signs of nearby civilization.

"It is no use, Jean," Jacques said.

Jean continued to scour the barren beach looking for a small tree. If he could fashion two poles and tie his coat to them, he would have a travois to drag Jacques inland. After searching several hundred yards up and down the shoreline with not even a scrub pine to show for it, he was shuffling sadly back to his injured friend when he suddenly saw a ship about a mile out in the gulf sailing leisurely in his direction.

Jean told Jacques he would swim to the sailing ship for

help. Too weak to stop him, Jacques stared in horror as his friend plunged into the surf. After he lost sight of him Jacques fixed his eyes on the slow-moving sailing ship for more than an hour before seeing a dinghy coming towards the beach. Jean had miraculously intercepted the Dutch vessel heading for New Orleans and brought back aid.

In a letter many years later Clemorgan recounted this incident, saying he owed every year of life beyond age twenty-one to his Negro companion from Haiti.

New Orleans bustled with activity, its harbor piers packed with cargo ships that would transport to France the mounds of cotton, timber, furs, sugar cane, and other products funneling into the city from the interior of the continent. The city itself teemed with shops, inns, crowds of busy people. An air of prosperity and gaiety hung over the gulf port. The French were indeed drawing wealth from their rich Louisiana territory.

But for Jean duSable there was one dreaded difference between Haiti and New Orleans. Few black men were free in this city. Between the Spanish influence and the wealthy French plantation owners, almost all Negroes labored in servitude. The two young Haitians had reached New Orleans penniless, without friends, and though poverty presented no legal problem for Jacques Clemorgan for Jean it meant he might be claimed as anyone's runaway slave. He had lost everything in the hurricane, including his papers to French citizenship.

Jacques, an intelligent white man, quickly obtained a job as clerk in one of New Orleans' merchandising houses, but Jean, despite his mental and physical abilities, could find nothing. He finally stumbled into a Catholic mission. Here he met a sympathetic priest, Father Pierre Gibault, who offered Jean room and board in exchange for maintaining the mission's grounds and buildings. Jean gratefully accepted. However, he could not keep himself from sulking, sometimes, because he could not find a better-paying job. His moodiness saddened Father Gibault, but Jean's compassion for the poor who came into the mission impressed him.

"Take heart, my son," the mission priest said to the dejected duSable. "You possess the sense of understanding and love for others that is too seldom seen in New France. God plans great things for you if you do not become bitter."

Jean, a devout Catholic, took heart from the priest's words and kept his faith in God.

He spent almost a year at the mission house in New Orleans. Occasionally he wrote his father saying he was doing well as a merchant, too proud and stubborn to admit that he needed financial help. Though his father knew of Jean's problems because Jacques Clemorgan had written the truth home, he sent no money nor asked for his son's return to the plantation. Such an action might insult Jean, brand him a failure in his own eyes. The elder duSable simply sent Jean a copy of his French citizenship papers.

In New Orleans white men in prominent jobs did not associate openly with blacks. Jacques wanted to see more of his black friend but Jean refused, fearing that a close association might cost Clemorgan his position as clerk.

In February, 1765, while Jean puttered about the mission garden, a tall leather-faced Indian trudged into the yard, appearing so tired and weak that Jean led him to a bench under a magnolia tree. The Indian, a Potawatomi named Choctaw, originally from the Great Lakes region, had traveled the length of the Mississippi River many times in his work as a guide for fur traders. In his last job he had met with injustice. After arriving in New Orleans, his employer dismissed the Indian with no money when they finished delivering their furs to a buyer. Choctaw could do nothing. Who in this city would believe Choctaw instead of his white employer? So, penniless, he had been roving through the streets, grubbing for food wherever he could find or steal it. On this particular day, he had wandered into the mission grounds.

When Father Gibault heard the Indian's story he frowned

and Jean thought the priest disliked the idea of caring for another pauper. Somewhat irritated, he offered to share with the Indian his own daily ration of food.

Father Gibault smiled. "My son, you have the compassion that Christ wishes in all men. But you misunderstand. I frown in disappointment because this man, one of God's children as are all of us, has been deprived of his dignity by those who practice hypocrisy."

"I'm sorry, Father," Jean said.

"Perhaps our visitor can assist you in the garden," Father Gibault said, "so that he may earn his keep the same as you."

For the next several days, Choctaw followed Jean about like a domesticated shepherd dog, working at whatever chore he assigned to him. But Choctaw looked upon Jean as a curiosity, never before having seen a black man who was not a slave, nor one who showed so much intelligence and self-assurance.

Jean, too, was curious. Choctaw attended Mass regularly and knew his Catholic prayers. Jean learned that the Potawatomi Indians, who lived on the shores of Lake Michigan, had been influenced by early French missionaries. The "Black Robes" had Christianized the Potawatomi tribe on the banks of the St. Joseph River in Michigan during the late seventeenth and early eighteenth centuries. Priests like Father Charlevoix and Father Allouez had carried on the initial missionary efforts of Father Marquette until the eruption of vicious Indian wars among the Great Lakes tribes had forced them to flee for their lives. The Potawatomi Indians had continued for the past fifty years to carry on the rituals of the Black Robes without the presence of Catholic priests.

Besides the explanation of his Christian background, Choctaw talked of other things. He spoke of the freedom in the northern wilderness—no slaves and no masters—and of the beautiful rivers and lakes, the sea of plains, the endless forests. Finally, Choctaw spoke of the riches in furs awaiting those strong enough to hunt for them.

Jean duSable listened intently, fascinated. Before long, the

16

Negro decided that fur trapping in the wondrous lands to the north offered a profitable and adventurous future. He asked Choctaw if they could make a fur trapping expedition together, but the Indian had a good answer, How could they go anywhere when they did not have a sou between them?

The determined Jean duSable made one of his rare visits to his white friend from Haiti. Jacques Clemorgan listened breathlessly, hanging onto every excited word. Yes, Jacques told Jean, he would be more than happy to lend him the money, not only paying for a dug-out canoe but buying traps, guns, and whatever else was needed for the venture. Jean declined such generosity, stating he did not want Jacques to lend out his total savings. Jacques answered with a grin and then said that he would accompany them.

When Jean frowned, Jacques laughed, "After all, I must protect my investment. Besides, my body grows fat from sitting at this desk day after day, and my mind dull from answering yes to my employer at the stroke of every hour."

Father Gibault offered the three men his blessings and gave them what food he could spare, some cooking utensils and blankets. When Jean promised to repay the good father, the mission priest simply gestured.

"Repay God with good works."

So it was that in February of 1765 three men—one white, one black, and one red—began the long 600-mile paddle up the Mississippi River to the French settlement of St. Louis.

Chapter Three

A Frenchman, Pierre Loclade Liquest, the first man to settle above the Mississippi River on the bluffs that one day became St. Louis, in 1762 formed a fur trading company in New Orleans. Then, after the Louisiana governor granted him rights to trade with the Missouri Indians, Liquest went northward and established himself on the bluffs just below the junction of the Missouri and Mississippi rivers. French merchants resented his monopoly on the fur trade, so within two years the French government opened the entire area to all fur trappers. Few had taken advantage of the new policy. When Jean and Jacques arrived there in 1765 St. Louis included only several log cabins, all of them belonging to French trappers.

Jean and Jacques, with the help of Choctaw, immediately felled timber and built a rude cabin of their own on the bluffs above the Mississippi. Then the three men paddled up the Missouri in search of martens. The experienced Choctaw taught the Haitians how to set traps, where to find martens, and how to strip fur from the animals without harming the pelt. The Haitians, intelligent and willing, learned fast and quickly accustomed themselves to the harsh, often cold, climate. By the time the expedition ended they had proven themselves as durable in the wilderness as Choctaw. The trio returned to St. Louis in May with two fine bundles of marten pelts.

To their surprise they found the hamlet crowded with rudely clad Indian and French trappers as well as store-dressed buyers. They had not realized St. Louis became a busy place after spring trapping, that merchants from New Orleans came north in droves to bargain. Disappointingly, they also learned that pelts brought low prices in the St. Louis settlement because of the oversupply.

Choctaw suggested that Jean and Jacques take their pelts to New Orleans where buyers would pay twice the price as these buyers in St. Louis. But if they spent their time going back and forth to New Orleans, Jacques complained, they would have little time for trapping. Jean duSable agreed. So they planned a two-fold business. Jean, with the help of Choctaw, would spend his time trapping in the wilderness while Jacques Clemorgan devoted his to hauling the pelts downstream to New Orleans. Under this plan they could only spend a few months a year together, but they would get fine prices for their pelts.

For the next four years the two men worked as a trapping and selling team, with Choctaw their employee. Jean trekked off twice a year—in the fall and in the spring—to trap martens and beavers, then Clemorgan paddled off to New Orleans in January and June to sell the pelts. During this period both men gained experience and ability, with each new trip up the Missouri, Jean trapping more animals and returning with bigger and better pelts, Jacques in turn establishing a steady clientele of satisfied buyers in New Orleans. Neither of them had forgotten Father Pierre Gibault's Catholic mission; as they earned more the partners donated more money to it every time Jacques made a trip south.

Besides gathering pelts of their own they opened a trading

post in St. Louis, Jacques bringing back from New Orleans axes, powder, food, and other items to sell to the frontiersmen and Indians. In turn, they bought pelts from the Illinois, Ottawa, Miami tribes and from French trappers who came to St. Louis. Since Jacques made regular trips to New Orleans, anyway, he didn't care how many bundles of pelts he carried with him.

The Indians in the St. Louis area, much surprised, found an unexpected honesty in their dealings with the two young men. They were paid in goods or money at the same rate paid French trappers. As a result Indian trappers flocked to the Haitians' trading post and the business thrived. Neither duSable nor Clemorgan saw any reason to indulge in the common double standard, one for the Indian, one for the white men, or to short-change the red men. Jean's conscience would not allow him to cheat another human being and Clemorgan admired his sense of justice.

Because of Jean's fairness, his respect for the Indian, he gained many Indian friends around the St. Louis area, among them none other than Chief Pontiac, the retired leader of the Great Lakes Ottawa nation. Pontiac had been the scourge of the Midwest, especially against the English trying to expand westward from the Ohio valley frontier. After years of fighting the British, however, the great chief finally suffered two bad defeats, and in 1766 Sir William Johnson forced him to make peace. The aging Pontiac retired to Cahokia, a small Indian village just north of St. Louis, and agreed never to fight again. Between 1766 and 1769 Jean duSable made frequent trips to Cahokia to spend time with Pontiac. A great friendship developed between these two nonwhites. Pontiac was so impressed with Jean's love and respect for all men regardless of culture or race that he gave Jean an honor belt, the greatest tribute an Ottawa chief could bestow.

By 1769 St. Louis had grown into a busy fur-trading community. An inn, two saloons, livery stables and two general stores had sprouted on the bluff along with the cabin homes and trading posts of residents. Although Jean duSable and Jacques Clemorgan had established a fine trade, Jean and

Choctaw continued to make two yearly trapping expeditions into the upper Missouri wilderness.

When Jean returned from spring trapping in May, 1769, he found a disturbing change in St. Louis. The settlement bustled with its usual activity. Crowds of men still moved busily about the river bank or atop the barges returning from spring trapping. The dusty streets still teemed with unshaven trappers and their Indian guides. But the buyers in St. Louis this spring wore unfamiliar long-flowing coats, widebrimmed hats, and rich silk shirts. With these merchants were *black* men—perspiring shirtless toilers who carried the loads of furs from the riverbank to the warehouses on the bluffs above the river. Jean gaped in astonishment. Spaniards had come to St. Louis —bringing their slaves with them.

The dismayed duSable would not allow a single Spanish buyer to board his fur-laden barge to inspect his pelts. When he scampered up the bluff to his trading post, he fumed at Jacques.

"What are these Spaniards doing here?"

Sadly, Jacques explained. During Jean's absence in the wilderness, news had come that France had ceded Louisiana to Spain, the king having made a secret treaty at Fontainebleau. Louisiana was now a Spanish colony. French Governor D'Abbedie had already turned over the reins of government to his Spanish successor, Antonio deIlloe. Spanish merchants now controlled the Louisiana trade and trappers must deal with them.

The news infuriated Jean duSable and he angrily refused to sell his pelts.

"Never! Never will I deal with the Spaniards!" he shouted to Clemorgan.

"Jean," Clemorgan pleaded, "don't let your temper destroy all we've built for the past four years."

"No!" Jean cried sharply. "The Spaniards killed my mother. I'll have nothing to do with them!" His face flushed with anger. The fists of his big hands were tightly clenched and his strong muscular body was as rigid as a pole.

The two young men had occasionally argued, for even the

21

best of friends can not agree on everything. Jacques had grown accustomed to Jean's hot temper and in the past had always managed to calm him down. But this time he was not sure he could. The anger in Jean's brown eyes blazed like hot coals.

"Jean, please," Jacques pleaded again.

"No!"

Then the Negro stormed into their business place, leaving a distressed Clemorgan standing in front of the trading post. He looked at their barge tied up on the river and irritably rubbed his face. The cargo of pelts was the finest load Jean had ever brought back; even from his position on the bluff Jacques could see the sheen of the marten pelts in the afternoon sun. They could bring the best price ever and Jacques could not bear the thought of losing such a sale. Worse, he would disappoint several New Orleans buyers and injure his reputation in the gulf port city. He suddenly scowled and scuffed the ground in front of their log trading post. It was not his fault that France had ceded New Orleans and the Mississippi valley to the Spaniards.

Jean duSable soon realized that he could not stubbornly deprive Jacques of his own labors. He apologized to his white partner and told him to sell the furs to whomever it pleased him, but he himself would never again gather furs in the wilderness to warm the heads and shoulders of Spaniards.

No amount of pleading or reasoning could change Jean's mind. He sulked for several days, unwilling to listen to either Jacques or Choctaw. Jacques had hoped that Jean would accept the Spanish control of the Mississippi valley and be able to live with it, but Jean refused to reconsider his decision. Then what would he do? Jean said he would leave Louisiana altogether, go where there was no Spanish tyranny, British authority, or other injustice against men.

"You seek a dream, Jean duSable," Clemorgan told him. "There is no such place."

But strangely enough, an act of treachery gave Jean the opportunity to seek this dream. He was nibbling at his supper,

22

still brooding ten days later, when a runner from Cahokia entered the cabin in St. Louis to tell him that Chief Pontiac wanted to see him at once. Jean frowned in surprise. Pontiac knew that he always visited Cahokia as soon as he finished his business in St. Louis. Why did Pontiac need to see him right now? Jean asked the runner.

A surge of bitterness wrinkled the Indian's face before he answered, "What the British could not accomplish in battle against the Great Pontiac they have accomplished with treachery."

Then the Ottawa said that Pontiac had been stabbed in his sleep by an Illinois brave who had come to Cahokia disguised as an Ottawa, apparently sent by the British to assassinate him and thus rekindle a Great Lakes war between the Ottawas and the Illinois. The dishonorable Illinois brave had crept into Pontiac's lodge in the dead hours of the night and plunged a knife into the chief's breast. Pontiac, certain his days were numbered, had asked to see duSable and Choctaw before he died.

The horrifying news shook Jean duSable as nothing else could. He prepared at once to leave for Cahokia. Jacques Clemorgan, though distressed by the attack on Pontiac, saw the incident as a blessing in disguise. Jean, eager to help the aged chief, had left his brooding shell, the sudden tragedy erasing a lesser problem—like selling furs to the Spaniards.

Jacques watched in relief as Jean rode off with Choctaw and the Ottawa. By the time He returned to St. Louis he would have spent his anger against the Spaniards.

However, at this moment in May, 1769, neither Jacques Clemorgan nor Jean duSable could guess that the visit to Cahokia would bring a great change in the life of Jean Baptiste Pointe duSable, foreshadowing the prophecy made by Father Pierre Gibault four years ago: *God plans great things for you, my son.*

23

Chapter Four

War had been a way of life for the past half century in the Midwest, so all Indian nations desired chiefs who were warriors with daring, prowess, and ability. Pontiac possessed these qualities. The Ottawas had welcomed him as chief in 1755, after his father died.

No Ottawa chieftain had ever before inherited such problems. Not only did he face continuing warfare with the Miami, Sac, and Illinois tribes, he also faced the British who had elbowed their way into the Midwest. The Indians had lived easily with the handful of French trappers who merely took furs and then returned to New Orleans or Quebec, but the British wanted land—Indian land—to start farms and settlements.

The invasion of British homesteaders into the Ohio valley during the 1750's brought an angry response from the Ottawas. Pontiac first scourged several Miami tribes who had made territorial peace treaties with England. Then while they still reeled from the powerful Ottawa assaults he had led his determined war parties in attacks against several British forts, mauled the redcoat columns sent westward to find him and finally, during the French and Indian War, led the attack that nearly destroyed General James Braddock's army. So successful were the Ottawas that their traditional Illinois enemies joined the fierce Pontiac in an all-out war to drive the British from the Midwest.

When France lost the French and Indian War in 1763 the British sent hordes of soldiers and volunteers from their settlements in the Ohio valley into the Midwest to fight the bitterly anti-British Pontiac. There were three years more of vicious skirmishes. The superior British forces slowly turned the tide, the Illinois tribes quit the fight and sought peace with the British, and the French failed to send Pontiac the military help promised. The British could not be dislodged from Detroit and Pontiac retreated southward, losing several fights along the way. After a bad defeat at Kaskaskia he surrendered to Sir William Johnson on July 25, 1766, agreeing never to fight again, and retired to Cahokia, a place he had come to love during his fighting years in the Mississippi valley. He turned the Ottawa leadership over to his son who ruled the tribe from St. Clair on the shores of Lake Huron.

Chief Pontiac's camp at Cahokia, twenty-five miles north of St. Louis, sat on a high peninsula where the Cahokia River joined the wide Mississippi. The fifty Ottawas with him at the camp, like Choctaw, came from the Great Lakes region, sent by the Ottawa nation in homage to Pontiac for the sole purpose of serving and caring for him.

As usual, Indians crowded the center of Cahokia as Jean duSable rode into camp. They generally greeted him with smiles and gestures, but today they appeared quiet. No children danced around his prancing horse, no squaws glanced up from their basket weaving to smile, no braves argued playfully among themselves for the honor of taking the reins of Jean's horse. The Indians at Cahokia were obviously in mourning.

Jean and Choctaw walked directly to Pontiac's lodge. They found him lying on a bearskin cot dressed in the rich dress of an Ottawa chieftain. The carefully woven coat sparkled with the painted emblems of the various Ottawa tribes. The wide belt was draped across his shoulder etched with designs of lakes and mountains, the domains over which Pontiac had ruled. But the chief's face, pale and gaunt, showed a deathly yellow color.

Pontiac greeted the Negro with a weak smile and then extended a trembling hand. Jean gripped it and squeezed the chief's arm in sympathy, never having expected to see the great Pontiac lying like a helpless child. He managed to smile but Pontiac noticed the deep gloom in his dark eyes.

"I can see that you mourn for me. Do not grieve, dear friend, for I have lived an honorable life. Many years did I lead my people against our enemies, Indian and British alike. Our people remain strong and proud. Our numbers are greater than those of any other Indian nation. I shall go willingly when the Great Spirit calls."

Jean tried to comfort the dying chieftain and assure him that he would recover from the assassin's knife wounds. Pontiac feebly shook his head. His hours were numbered. He had called Jean hastily to Cahokia because great trouble would befall the midwestern Indians after his death, his passing trigger the worst bloodshed ever seen on the continent. Even now the powerful Ottawas were preparing to ravage Illinois and Miami tribes. They would kill, loot, and destroy in a mad desire for revenge. The Miami and Illinois, out of necessity, would strike back and Ottawas pay a heavy toll in dead braves and counterattacks on their own villages.

Pontiac twisted his face in agony over the prospect of such a bloodbath, and his deathly white face looked even more ghastly.

Choctaw, kneeling next to the dying Pontiac, bowed in homage, and took his hand. "It must be so, Honored Chief. Even the neutral Potawatomis will act because of this treachery. They will help the Ottawas to avenge this foul deed against the great Pontiac."

Pontiac, however, shook his head. Then, shuttling his

glance between Choctaw and Jean duSable, he weakly spoke again. "During these days of lying on my deathbed I have had many hours to think about myself, about my people, and about the Indian nations of this continent. I have concluded that the time has come to stop these senseless wars among the nations of the Great Lakes. I tremble at the thought of a bloodbath because of the treacherous deed against me by a few selfish men. Unless a calming voice speaks the Indian nations will destroy themselves. They will play into the hands of the traitorous British who will trample over the bloodied dead of Indian braves to occupy the Great Lakes." Pontiac pointed feebly at Jean duSable. "Dearest friend, I ask that you arrange a peace treaty among the Ottawas, Miamis, and Illinois tribes. Go to the camp of the Potawatomis on the St. Joseph River and ask them to host such a council of peace on their neutral lands."

Choctaw gaped in astonishment. Surely, the mortal wounds had affected the mind of the great chief. The Ottawas had always been great warriors, with Pontiac the bravest among them. Every male child, from the day he was able to understand, lived for the day he could join a war party against his centuries-old enemies. And now, the Great Pontiac would forgive the treacherous attack on his life.

Jean, meanwhile, felt a sense of panic. How could he accomplish what others had failed to accomplish for centuries? How, especially, would he do this when even now a cry for revenge rose from every Ottawa village? Jean had seen the hostility and mistrust in the eyes of every Illinois and Ottawa who chanced to meet at his trading post. The hatred was imbedded in their very hearts. No one could remove it. Jean, unwilling to make a pledge he could not keep, told Pontiac he did not think he had the power to bring about such a treaty.

Pontiac's eyes gleamed. He appeared more pleased than disappointed with Jean's reply. He had again proven his integrity: not even to a dying man would he lie, no matter how comforting the lie might be. The chief smiled and motioned

Jean to come closer. When the young man knelt next to him Pontiac pointed to the honor belt girding Jean's waist. He reminded him that few men had ever received this prize from an Ottawa chief, and that only after many pondering months had he himself become certain that duSable truly respected and loved the Indian, and so deserved the belt which would command respect in any Ottawa or Potawatomi village covering the wide lands to the north. It would even bring esteem from the Miami and Illinois, their Ottawa enemies. Pontiac finally reminded Jean that at his trading post in St. Louis he dealt with Miami and Illinois Indians as well as Ottawas and with his white partner evidenced high regard for the Indians by dealing fairly with them.

Jean admitted he had always tried to deal honestly with all fellow humans.

"True," Pontiac said to Jean. "And you have gained the respect of all Indians in the Midwest. You are the most respected non-Indian in the Mississippi valley. If anyone can bring peace to the Great Lakes it is you. The Indians will listen to you above all others."

Such a peace treaty would not come easily, he warned. Jean would find the Ottawa leaders devoting all energy to seeking vengeance against the Illinois, and he must not only convince them not to fight but persuade them to invite Miami and Illinois chieftains to a peace council. If he could convince the Ottawas he would have an excellent chance. The Ottawas were, after all, the most powerful of the Great Lakes nations and could move from a position of strength. Would Jean go to the St. Joseph and ask the chief of the Potawatomis to arrange a peace council? Would he speak at this council?

Jean agreed, but said he could not guarantee anything. Pontiac smiled weakly, satisfied that he would try, and said he himself could die easily now, knowing he had done all he could to save the Midwest from self-destruction.

Pontiac next turned to Choctaw and asked the Indian to take Jean to the camp on the St. Joseph River. He would know the route, how to avoid enemies—they'd be traveling through Illinois and Miami country—also how to provision for the long journey. Choctaw answered that he would not only take Jean to St. Joseph, but swear to his Potawatomi chief that the great Pontiac himself had sent the young trader on this peace mission.

The chief asked that Jean leave immediately, the mission to St. Joseph being more important than his own impending death or even a final period of companionship.

In St. Louis Jacques Clemorgan offered no objections to Jean's peace mission. He welcomed it. He helped Jean and Choctaw to stock a dugout canoe for the trip, loading clothing, axes, coffee, flour for biscuits, dried and salted meat, blankets, and canvas for shelter. Finally, they packed muskets with plenty of powder and musket balls.

At the time of departure, two days later, word came that the great Chief Pontiac had died. Sadness was reflected in Jean's big dark eyes, his whole body aching from a mixture of sorrow and anger. Jacques, hoping to lift his spirits, told him he could find comfort in his mission to the Great Lakes, the change would do him good, and when he returned he would be ready to work again. Jean did not answer his partner. His face remained hard and his eyes bitter as he slammed supplies into the dugout.

Jacques panicked. "Jean, don't do anything foolish," he pled. "You *will* come back?"

"You're my dearest friend, Jacques," Jean finally answered. "You know I'd give my life for you, but I can take no more of this Spanish oppression or English treachery. If I find a place where men can live in freedom and peace, where men can enjoy equality. . . ."

"You're talking nonsense," Jacques interrupted. "You're looking for something that exists only in good men's dreams. I know you're bitter and angry now, but don't throw away four years of hard work. Think carefully, Jean. Promise me you won't do anything foolish."

29

But Jean could not. He tightly gripped Jacques' hand, kissed him on both cheeks in the French tradition of honored friendship, and said only, "Good-by, dearest friend."

Jacques Clemorgan's heart sank as he watched Jean push his canoe away from the sandy shore, fearing he might never see his lifelong partner again. He stood on the riverbank, squinting, until the canoe faded into the distance, then sighed and walked sadly back to their cabin on the bluff.

By mid afternoon the twenty-four-year-old Jean duSable and his Indian companion had passed the junction of the Missouri and Mississippi Rivers. When they reached the Cahokia River Jean, squinting at the lodges of Pontiac's camp, saw Indians moving large stones, apparently preparing Pontiac's funeral tomb.

The two men paddled upriver for the rest of the day, then stopped for the night some ten miles above Cahokia, made camp and tied their canoe under some dense overhanging branches, out of sight of any dishonest trappers or foraging Indians who might run off with it during the night.

By noon the next day they left the Mississippi River and turned northeastward up the Illinois. Jean, now forgetting his anger with the Spaniards and his sorrow for Pontiac, stared like a curious child at lands he had never seen before. The tall pine forests ran from the shoreline of the Illinois River to the distant hills. Occasional herds of buffalo thundered across the prairie. The riverbank villages had strange markings on their teepees, and the inhabitants, tall and straight, stood on the shoreline and looked coldly at the passing canoe.

Choctaw explained that these solemn-faced Indians were Illinois who claimed as their own all the lands that bordered the Illinois River. They resented anyone who traveled through this country but, as was the custom of all midwestern Indians, they accepted the river as a natural waterway open to anyone. Thus, although they stood on the riverbank and glared, the Indians made no attempt to enter the river and bother the two men.

For several days Jean and Choctaw continued up the Illi-

30

nois River, passing more villages where more Indians glared at them from the riverbanks, more pine forests and rolling prairies. When they passed the great Illinois village of Peoria and came into Miami country, Choctaw grew nervous. Jean expressed surprise. The Miami, mostly farmers and trappers, were not half as warlike as the Illinois or Ottawa. But Choctaw explained that their peaceful nature itself made them dangerous. The Miamis had suffered so many attacks from Illinois, Ottawa and Sac war parties that they were suspicious of strangers and would act quickly if either Choctaw or Jean showed the slightest sign of hostility. He warned Jean to disregard the villagers standing on the riverbanks; if they ignored the Indians the Indians would ignore them.

Another week passed before the two men left behind the Illinois River and Miami country. They had been traveling upriver for nearly two weeks and every muscle in Jean's body ached, his legs had stiffened from being cramped inside the canoe and blisters had broken out on his hands from the days of paddling. That night when they camped the weary duSable all but collapsed on his blanket.

How much further was it to the St. Joseph? Another week, Choctaw answered. They would reach the Eschikagou portage tomorrow. From there, they would paddle along the south shore of Lake Michigan, then trek northward overland to the St. Joseph River and the main camp of the Potawatomi Indians.

The next day they started northeastward up narrow Des Plaines River until they reached a new kind of country. Jean looked about in surprise. The terrain on either side of the river stretched wide and flat out of sight in all directions, reminding him of the flat marshes around New Orleans.

A day later on a cool morning in May, 1769, as the canoe slipped through the marshes, the young Negro gaped in awe. A far different landscape greeted him. Flowers of every color and description covered the wide flat plains beyond the riverbanks. He saw patches of violets, fields of buttercups, swaying bluebells, and huge fields of long-stemmed plants with pink flowers at their heads. Everywhere around, the air was perfumed. Along the riverbanks beavers and otters scurried in and out of the water by the hundreds. Beyond the shoreline of Des Plaines River, soil as black as coal itself covered the terrain, rich virgin land seeming to cry for a farmer's plow. At the north end of the plains thick pine, maple, and spruce forests offered a wide variety of accessible lumber.

As he and Choctaw pulled their canoe from the water and strapped supplies to their backs, Jean continued to stare at the flat land about him. He had traveled the length of the Mississippi River and far up the Missouri River wilderness, he had known the Caribbean area and been to France, but never before had he seen a land so rich in color, small game, and earth. Crops and livestock would thrive here. The game would bring abundant fur, and the easy reaches of timber would speed the construction of buildings.

"This land is beautiful," he said to his companion. "But why is there no settlement, not even an Indian village, on this wonderful plain?"

Choctaw agreed that the Eschikagou plain was indeed rich and beautiful land, with furs so plentiful one could trap otters two at a time. The earth would grow anything from maize to alfalfa. But, Choctaw said, Eschikagou was a centuries-old battleground. No one used the Eschikagou portage because of war parties; for the same reason, no one dared to settle here. Most people followed the safer route down the Ohio valley on the long journey between Quebec and New Orleans.

"I cannot believe that God would deprive honest and grateful men of the opportunity to build a settlement here," Jean said.

Choctaw shrugged and then pointed to some of the beaten paths that criss-crossed the plains—the trails of Indian war parties—reminding Jean that French and British explorers had tried for two centuries to establish a settlement here. The war parties that constantly roamed the Eschikagou plain had always driven them back. If a raiding Indian band found anyone here not of its tribe, he was considered an enemy who would not live to see another sunset. Even the name of the plain, Eschikagou, was born from battle. Many centuries ago, according to the Ottawas, a noble chieftain named Eschikagou defeated the Illinois on this plain in one of the greatest victories of Ottawa history. The Indians named the plains after him.

Carrying their canoe and their supplies Jean and Choctaw plodded for two leagues over the plains. As they moved across the portage Jean's eyes darted in every direction. The Eschikagou plain had entranced him. He continued to look in fascination at the beautiful surroundings and, by the time they reached the shore of Lake Michigan to stop for rest, Jean had made up his mind. Indian battleground or not, he would build on this barren plain.

In his mind, Jean was already planning a settlement. He would plant alfalfa in this area, graze cattle in that area, and seed an orchard in another. He would build a road across the two-league plain from Lake Michigan to Des Plaines River. He could then transport travelers and their supplies by cart and oxen across the portage. And finally he studied the strange way the river's two channels, like a Y, ran into a third that flowed into Lake Michigan. At the mouth of this river he would build his house.

When Jean told Choctaw of his plans the Indian grunted. He admired Jean's eagerness, but doubted that the Ottawas or any other tribe would listen to Jean's pleas for peace. The Ottawas not only would make war but would, no doubt, use the age-old Eschikagou battleground for their staging area. Already the Ottawas were seeking Illinois blood. Choctaw warned Jean to stop daydreaming and move on. If any war parties were roving the plain at this moment, they might kill first and then decide whether Jean and Choctaw had been friends or foes.

As they loaded their canoe and started out from the beach, Jean once more stared hungrily at the beautiful portage. His eyes sparkled excitedly. If he could really bring peace among the Indian nations of the Midwest, he could safely build a cabin on the Eschikagou plain.

Suddenly, Jean duSable was eager to reach the St. Joseph River.

Chapter Five

Choctaw and Jean duSable hugged the shoreline of Lake Michigan to avoid the high waves rolling across the middle. Lake Michigan, a huge body of fresh water stretching north to a blue horizon, was the same deep blue as the Caribbean, reminding the Haitian of the sea at home, though the taste of the clear water contrasted sharply. And unlike the huge waves that exploded on the shores of the Caribbean, Lake Michigan broke in ripples against the forested shoreline, and the stiff breeze whipping across its vast surface carried a piercing chill instead of the comforting West Indian warmth.

On the shoreline birch trees stood thickly, like massed white poles with branches of sprouting spring buds resembling clinging flakes of snow. Beyond the birches, dense spruce and firs rose in straight majestic height, nothing like the bunched gnarled brakes of the Caribbean. The forest floor surprised Jean, too, appearing clean and smooth with only an occasional pine cone dotting the surface, a terrain far different from the overgrown underbrush of tropical rain forests.

After two more days of paddling close to the shore, Jean

and Choctaw reached a cove on the east where Choctaw hid the dugout under some overhanging branches. Then they strapped their supplies to their backs and started northward towards the St. Joseph River, over Indian trails that wound through the thick birch and pine brakes. Except for the occasional screech of a bird, the two men saw or heard nothing. Jean wondered why no Indians had stopped or interfered with them. They were deep in Potawatomi country. Choctaw assured him that Indians would show themselves at the proper time. Potawatomi braves had probably watched them on Lake Michigan and no doubt were following their progress through the forest.

On the third day after leaving Lake Michigan they finally emerged from the edge of the forest. Choctaw pointed towards the settlement in the St. Joseph valley beyond. Even from this distance the camp appeared huge. Dozens of Indians moved busily about the settlement. A few hundred yards east of it lay the remains of an old French fort, north of which was an abandoned mission church. As the two men moved along a path through the wild valley grass Choctaw warned Jean to stay alert, to expect to meet Indians at any moment, to make no move towards his weapon.

When they came within several hundred yards of the St. Joseph camp several Indians jumped suddenly from the brush, surrounding and menacing them with bows and arrows, but making no effort to really harm the weary travelers.

"Hold," Choctaw told the leader of the Indian band. "I am Choctaw, a Potawatomi who returns from the Father of Waters. This," he gestured toward his companion, "is Jean duSable, the blood brother of Pontiac. See the honor belt around his waist."

The leader studied the black man from head to foot and then his eyes locked on the gold-studded belt girding Jean's waist. He motioned to the other Indians to lower their weapons.

"We come from the Great Pontiac's camp at Cahokia," Choctaw said. "He sent this man to speak to your chief."

The head of the Indian band nodded, then, gesturing with

a quick jerk of his arm, led Jean and Choctaw across the open valley towards the camp. Within a few minutes they were walking between the orderly rows of birch bark lodges, crowds of Indians staring at the strangers, especially the dark-skinned Jean duSable. Squaws stopped their work and looked up, children sheltering themselves next to them, and elderly men and women studied them curiously while Indian braves straightened and glared.

Jean glanced about the huge sprawling settlement. Young braves were fashioning stone arrowheads or stringing bows with what might have been buffalo tendons. Other men sharpened battle axes or were making tomahawks from flat stones and tree limbs. Jean frowned. The Potawatomis were preparing for war.

Jean and Choctaw were led to a bark longhouse, the largest structure in the settlement. Totem poles flanked its entrance and the painted figure of an elk—emblem of the Potawatomi tribe—hung above the doorway. The leader raised his hand, motioning the two visitors to wait. Then he disappeared inside the lodge. A moment later, a tall young Indian emerged from the longhouse, his muscular body held straight and erect as he shuttled his gleaming dark eyes between his visitors.

"I am Pokagon," the Indian said, "chief of the Potawatomi tribe at St. Joseph."

Jean pursed his lips in surprise. Pokagon seemed unusually young to be chief. His long, neatly combed hair hung to his shoulders and draped a narrow face, and a single feather stuck out of the blue-and-white checkered band that encircled his head. He was fully clothed in deerskin coat, trousers—and moccasins, with a blue-and-white-checkered shawl hung over his shoulders.

Choctaw told Pokagon that he and Jean had come from St. Louis, a trading-post center just below Pontiac's camp at Cahokia, that Jean duSable was a great friend of Pontiac who had sent him here to see the St. Joseph chief.

Chief Pokagon surprised Choctaw by telling him he had been expecting Jean's arrival ever since a runner had come from Cahokia two weeks ago to report Pontiac's death and a Jean duSable's coming. He looked at the honor belt and smiled, saying that only four men had ever received an honor belt from Pontiac, duSable being the only non-Indian. It proved beyond doubt that the great Pontiac had indeed considered him a favored one. Therefore, Pokagon welcomed him as a trusted brother to St. Joseph.

"Because of this cherished friendship with Pontiac, he sent me to speak to you," Jean said. "It was his wish that you listen to what he had to say."

The young chief placed a hand of friendship on Jean's shoulders, indicating to a nearby brave that the belongings of these guests were to be removed to the visitors' lodge and the lodge prepared for them. Jean and Choctaw unstrapped their backpacks and the Indian brave hurried off with them. Chief Pokagon motioned to the doorway of his own lodge, and inside to a thick buffalo rug. Pokagon sat crosslegged on it across from them, while the brave who had led them into camp standing stiffly behind him with folded arms, as though guarding the young chief from harm.

Pokagon once again gazed at Jean and Choctaw and then settle his gaze on Jean. He told him that the Potawatomis had detested the treacherous murder of Pontiac as much as their Ottawa friends. Therefore, the Potawatomis had agreed to help the Ottawas in an all-out war against the Illinois. Already, the Ottawas were extracting vengeance from the Illinois and the Potawatomis were preparing to join them in this fight. Within the next two or three days, Potawatomi and Ottawa chiefs from all over the Great Lakes area would arrive at St. Joseph to plan war strategy. Every brave, every squaw, even the children would work to avenge Pontiac's death. Pokagon himself had not had an idle moment since the runner's news of Pontiac's assassination, but since Jean had been an honored friend of the great chief he would grant him an audience despite his busy schedule.

Jean suddenly felt nervous. Instead of neutral ground the St. Joseph village had become a war camp against the Illinois. Having found a leader totally occupied with thoughts of revenge, Jean was disheartened. How could he, a Haitian and a Negro, talk of peace in this hostile Indian village? However, he was determined to keep his promise. Pontiac, he said, had made an urgent request before he died and hoped Pokagon and the other chiefs would abide by it. Pokagon gestured and promised to carry out Pontiac's last wishes if he could.

Jean exchanged glances with Choctaw.

"And what was Pontiac's request?" Pokagon asked.

Jean still hesitated for a moment. Then he took a deep breath. "The great chief, whose mind had been as clear as a swift stream in spite of his mortal wounds, asked," he said deliberately, "that you and the other chiefs make a peace treaty with the Illinois and Miami tribes. He asked that you hold a council of peace here on the St. Joseph."

Pokagon straightened his sinewy body with a jerk, his narrow face hardened, and he looked at Jean in disbelief. Then he squinted as though stunned. Even the leader standing behind him gaped in astonishment.

Choctaw suddenly spoke. "Jean speaks the truth, Pokagon. He brings this message in Pontiac's name. On my honor as a Potawatomi, with my own ears I heard the great chief on his deathbed. I first believed that the treacherous Illinois knife had mortally wounded his mind as well as his body. I could not believe that the Great Pontiac, who conquered and destroyed his enemies wherever he found them, would now ask that his people make peace with them. But," Choctaw raised his hand solemnly, "by the time we left his lodge, I was sure that Pontiac spoke wisely in seeking peace among the warring Great Lakes tribes."

"Do you know the mistrust that exists between the Ottawas and the Illinois?" Pokagon asked Jean.

Jean nodded. "I have seen the hate and suspicion between Ottawa and Illinois braves when they came to our trading post in St. Louis. But Pontiac knew it even more. He concluded that continued war among the Indians would only weaken the tribes so that the Indians of the Great Lakes could not protect themselves against greedy men. When the knife was plunged into his heart, he was more certain than ever that peace must prevail among the Indian nations."

"Remembering the character of Pontiac," Pokagon said, "I'm sure he had the courage to forgive as well as the courage to fight in battle."

Jean admitted himself being astonished at Pontiac's request for a peace treaty among these centuries-old Indian enemies, but the more he thought about it, the more he believed it would be in the interest of all the Great Lakes Indians.

Pokagon shook his head vigorously. He could not possibly fulfill this deathbed wish of Pontiac.

Jean reminded Pokagon that he was the chief of a powerful Indian nation generally neutral in the Great Lakes wars. Surely such a leader as he could influence a council of chiefs.

But still Pokagon declined. He had only just assumed the chieftainship of the Potawatomis following his father's recent death; the Potawatomi subchiefs had not yet officially proclaimed him chief. No one, he said, was likely to challenge his elevation when the council met in St. Joseph since under Potawatomi law a chief's son usually became chief when his father died. The council would act quickly; the council's main business was the serious business of war. Ottawa chiefs would come to St. Joseph with the Potawatomi subchiefs for these war preparations, looking to Pokagon to lead the alliance with the Ottawas in the campaign against ancient enemies. Did Jean seriously think that Pokagon could tell these chiefs to seek peace instead of war? How would it look if Pokagon's first act as the new chief was to ask for peace? No, it was impossible.

"You yourself said that Pontiac had the courage to forgive as well as the courage to fight," Jean said. "Does the new chief of the Potawatomis have any less courage than Pontiac?"

Pokagon's eyes suddenly flashed in anger. His face flushed. "I have never lacked courage," he barked. "If I thought so, I would not accept the chieftainship of my nation. It is simply that I have an obligation to my people. Every Potawatomi brave, every squaw, and every child has taken up the Ottawa cry for revenge against the Illinois. Would you call me wrong or cowardly to follow the wishes of my people?"

"You must believe me," Jean said. "Pontiac never spoke more wisely than he did on his deathbed. He, too, was only thinking of his people when he asked that I arrange a peace treaty among the Indians. It was his sincere belief that all the tribes, including the Ottawas, could remain strong only if they lived in peace with their surrounding neighbors."

"Perhaps," Pokagon said.

Jean pointed out that the British had carried out this foul deed against the great chief, buying the soul of this dishonorable Illinois just as, many years ago, other sinful men bought the soul of a wretch to betray Jean's own Christian God. Who would benefit if the Great Lakes Indians began a bloodbath that might turn red even the Father of Waters?

Pokagon said nothing but listened thoughtfully. Jean now warned him that the British looked on their lands with greedy eyes and, if the Indians sapped their strength in a bitter war, the British would surely march over their bones and take the lands. Did the brave who came to Jean in St. Louis speak the truth when he said: "What the British could not accomplish in battle against the Great Pontiac they have accomplished with teachery"? Jean begged Pokagon not to allow the red man's enemies to win with teachery that which they could not win in battle.

The Negro's powerful words erased the stern lines from Pokagon's face and softened the hard glint in his eyes. Even the brave standing behind him felt doubt after the stirring plea. Pokagon rose to his feet and placed a hand on the shoulder of the young Negro who had spoken eloquently, saying he now understood why Pontiac had given him an honor belt and placed his trust in him. He felt a true sympathy for his Indian brothers.

Jean's eyes brightened and he rose quickly to his feet. Would Pokagon then speak to the council?

Pokagon shook his head. He would not admit that he him-

41

self favored peace, but would allow Jean to speak to the council. The young chief would make no attempt to sway the council one way or the other. If Jean convinced them then Pokagon would act in the council's name and arrange a peace conference on the St. Joseph. Pokagon warned that should Jean persuade the Ottawa and Potawatomi chiefs he must also win the trust of the Illinois and Miamis. Such a task might be even more difficult.

Then he turned and walked slowly to the doorway of his longhouse to stand and stare silently into the daylight beyond.

Jean joined him and gripped his shoulder. "Pokagon, if peace comes, you will rule the Potawatomi nation during the most glorious time in its history."

Pokagon turned and faced Jean duSable. "Or I may be their chief during the most dishonorable time of our history," he said softly. "Now you must excuse me. I go to the chapel of the Black Robes to pray for guidance from the Great Spirit."

Jean, feeling a sudden heartbreak for him, did not answer as Pokagon left the lodge. He knew that the young chief now wrestled with his conscience, understanding that a fight to the death against the Illinois might well end with a conquest of his nation by the British. But on the other hand Pokagon was duty bound to carry out an all-out war against the enemy tribes.

For two days the drums echoed, the steady beats floating through the birch and pine forests south of the huge Potawatomi village, booming eastward along the length of the St. Joseph River, echoing up and down the eastern coast of Lake Michigan. The call to St. Joseph reached Potawatomi and Ottawa villages as far east as Lake Ontario, as far north as Lake Huron, and as far west as Lake Superior. By June 1, 1769, not only subchiefs from the Potawatomis, but also subchiefs from the Ojibwas, Chippewas, Hurons and other Ottawa tribes had funneled into St. Joseph.

The British at Detroit, Fort Niagara, and Fort Duquesne

soon learned of the council and, as they strengthened their outposts and called for reinforcements from the east, they gloated in satisfaction. The assassination of Pontiac had awakened a dragon stretching from Lake Ontario to Lake Superior —just as they had planned. Bands of braves from other nations would soon join the Ottawa war parties in the blind sweep against the Miami and Illinois tribes. The British need only wait until the Indians had spent themselves.

The call of chiefs to St. Joseph further aroused the Miami and Illinois tribes of the lower Great Lakes region. Already, because of Pontiac's murder Ottawa war parties had ravaged lands of the Illinois who now braced themselves for added hordes sure to come from the north on a rampage of revenge. The Miami, peaceful farmers, also suffering fanatic Ottawa attacks on their villages had of necessity, allied themselves with the Illinois to defend themselves against the expected scourge brewing in St. Joseph.

At the Potawatomi village itself, the Potawatomi subchiefs quickly finished their business of proclaiming Pokagon their new chief, not a single visitor to St. Joseph offering any objections, questioning him or putting him to the usual tests of skill in marksmanship, hunting, or wrestling. The ritual peace pipe passed quickly around the circle. The medicine men danced and chanted routinely as they asked the Great Spirit to guide the new chief in his reign. The buffalo roast festival ended earlier than usual and by ten o'clock in the evening of June 6, 1769, Pokagon officially donned the eagle feathered headdress of chieftain. The subchiefs and Ottawa guests simply offered quick congratulations. They had more pressing matters on their minds.

One of the council chiefs, an Ojibwa from Lake Huron, gripped the new chief's wrist. "Now, Pokagon, we retire to our lodge for tomorrow we begin grave business, the task of avenging the traitorous attack on the great Pontiac."

Other chiefs nodded agreement, rose from the circle and moved off to their lodges for the night. Pokagon turned to Jean duSable and asked him how he expected to discuss peace with these leaders who had come here to prepare for war. Jean could only repeat that he would try.

The following morning inside the large St. Joseph council house the subchiefs, again gathered in a circle crosslegged and waiting for the conference to begin, expressed surprise that Jean duSable was seated next to Pokagon. Some of them had noticed the stranger in camp but paid little attention to him, assuming he was simply a friendly trapper or trader. They waited curiously until Pokagon rose and looked about the circle.

"Great Council," Pokagon said, "with me is Jean duSable, a trader from St. Louis. He wears the honor belt given him by the great Pontiac. So much did Pontiac love and respect this man that on his deathbed he asked him to come to St. Joseph to speak with us. Let me only say that Jean duSable may be trusted as we would trust each other. I ask that this council listen."

A chain of mumbles ended when an Ottawa chief told Pokagon that the visitor who wore the honor belt of Pontiac should speak, asking only that the "white man" speak quickly since the council had important business of war.

Jean nervously rose to his feet and studied the somber faces in the wide circle. He spoke in the Potawatomi tongue, a language he had learned from Pontiac and Choctaw.

"Honored chiefs," he began, "the honor belt given to me by Pontiac is my most prized possession, for Pontiac was a great leader. I consider it a privilege to have been his close friend while he lived in Cahokia. Too many times to count did Pontiac and I hold long talks in his lodge. I learned from him the sacredness of trust that one man holds for another, and because of him tried always to show respect and fairness for all men, including the red man."

"All you say we accept," an Ottawa chief said impatiently, "but surely you have something more to say to this council."

"Yes. I come to you as I came to Chief Pokagon because Pontiac, on his deathbed, asked that I bring you his final

44

wish—that peace come to the Great Lakes tribes, and that you now make peace instead of war."

"Peace!" a subchief cried angrily. "Did the Illinois knife destroy the great Pontiac's mind even before the weapon destroyed his body? Would Pontiac really ask us to reward his murderers with peace?"

"His mind remained alive and alert," Jean answered. "Never did he speak more sincerely than he did on his deathbed."

Now he told them how clearly Pontiac had seen the intentions of the British in sending an Illinois assassin to murder Pontiac. If the council decided to scourge the other tribes of the Great Lakes it could not be done without weakening their own by the loss of many good braves and the destruction of many villages. For years the British had sought to take the Indian lands of the Great Lakes with their armies and guns, including those of the defeated General James Braddock, but found the Ottawas and Potawatomis too powerful. How better could the British win the lands they coveted than by pitting the northern Great Lakes tribes against the Illinois and Miamis? After the bloodshed they could move easily through the ravaged lands. DuSable warned the chiefs that the Spanish had now come to the Mississippi valley. Like vultures they would pick over whatever ground the British missed in trampling on the weakened Indian nations.

Only one Illinois brave had been involved in the terrible murder of Pontiac. Could the council chiefs blame the entire Illinois nation for the deeds of one Indian? Besides, did the chiefs think that the Illinois and Miami would not fight back? Even the most frightened coward will strike viciously when facing death or destruction. Jean asked an Ottawa chief if the Ottawas had so far escaped unharmed in their skirmishes with the Illinois. When the chief failed to answer Jean pointed sternly.

"You must admit—you *have* lost valuable braves. Are you not, then, playing into the hands of the British?"

The other chiefs waited soberly. Still the Ottawa leader did not answer. DuSable had spoken with power and conviction and the circle of Indian leaders now thought carefully, a few of them looking at Pokagon also thoughtfully pursing his lips. One asked him outright what he thought and the young Potawatomi chief answered that the council must make up its own mind. Pokagon, as host chief, would follow its wishes.

Jean, seeing the council waver, pushed his advantage. The council should fear no embarrassment or dishonor, he said, in seeking peace rather than war. Who could deny that Pontiac, who himself had fought harder and more bravely than any Great Lakes Indian, left a deadly fear in the hearts of the Illinois and Miami as well as in the hearts of the British? Did not the great chief speak wisely when he said the Ottawas were the strongest of all the Indian nations and could deal with other nations from a position of strength? Had not the Ottawas willingly followed him even at the risk of their lives? Would the council now ignore a request that the great Pontiac had made on his deathbed? A request made out of true love for his people? Was the honored chief not thinking of the Ottawas' welfare when he asked that the Great Lakes Indians deal with each other out of a sense of trust instead of a sense of suspicion?

The council chiefs were now listening intently to the Haitian Negro, sensing his sincerity. He certainly sought good for the Indian, not evil. They, like Pokagon, now understood why Pontiac had given duSable an honor belt.

"You are the host chief, Pokagon," one of the subchiefs said. "What say you to the black man's words?"

Pokagon, once more moved by the plea for peace, admitted that Jean duSable had spoken as a friend of the Indian. Perhaps Pontiac *had* spoken wisely on his deathbed. Perhaps the council *should* seek peace instead of war. Would it not be dishonorable for the Ottawas to ignore the deathbed wish of Pontiac having always followed the great chief while he lived?

Again there were nods from the council chiefs, and more

mumblings. Then, in a final homage to their departed chief, the Ottawa leaders agreed to seek peace. The man who wore the honor belt of Pontiac had convinced them. The medicine men were to pray to the Great Spirit and ask him to favor their decision.

When the council meeting ended Chief Pokagon placed a hand on Jean's shoulder.

"Jean duSable, I did not believe that you would persuade me or the council chiefs. You are a remarkable man. The Great Lakes needs such a calming hand as yours. Would you stay among us?"

"I'd like to build a cabin on the Eschikagou plain," Jean said. "It's so beautiful. But I'm told it's an Indian battle-ground."

"Always it has been so," Pokagon answered. "Many Frenchmen have attempted—unsuccessfully—to settle there. But," the young chief smiled, "if the Miami and Illinois chiefs listen to you as did the Ottawas on the council you may get your wish. Eschikagou would no longer be the eternal Indian battleground."

Chapter Six

Long before the white man ever heard of North America war played a part there just as it did in the civilized world. The Indians fought over hunting, fishing and grazing grounds, the Europeans over navigable rivers, habitable lands.

The Cherokees rose to power in southeastern North America. In the Southwest the Apaches and Utes overpowered other tribes. In the Northeast, the Iroquois became all-powerful. And by the middle of the eighteenth century the Ottawas, in territory stretching from the St. Lawrence River to Lake Superior, emerged with the strongest Indian claim on the continent.

Time had favored the Ottawas. Many historians agree that the Ottawas might have finally devoured the Miamis and Illinois and absorbed the Potawatomis except for the white man bringing his cunning and his guns to the New World. Like any group fighting another group, the Indians welcomed help from the white man, not realizing his true motive—conquest. England slowed the expansion of the Ottawa tribes in the Great Lakes area by aiding weaker tribes, in the process managing to weaken all the tribes of the Midwest at once. In the South and Southwest the Spaniards played off one tribe against another. Eventually, the Indian exhausted himself and the European invaders soon dominated North America.

Jean duSable's mission to the St. Joseph may have merely delayed the final downfall of the North American Indian.

Nevertheless, in 1769 Pokagon, the new chief of the Potawatomi nation, following the decision of the council, sent to the chiefs of Miami and Illinois tribes swift runners carrying invitations to attend a great midwestern parley at St. Joseph on the eastern shores of Lake Michigan. The Miami and Illinois leaders had expected plenty of war parties to swarm through their lands, not messengers. The tribes feared the Ottawas but they did not question the honor of the Potawatomis and quickly accepted the invitations, certain that Pokagon would not harm them. Talks would at least postpone certain defeat.

The sixteen chiefs chosen as representatives of these ancient Ottawa enemies found respect and comfort on their arrival at St. Joseph. Pokagon had warned his people to treat the visitors with courtesy. An Indian accepted his Chief's decision as the will of the Great Spirit, so, despite grim faces, there was no harassment.

Soon the visiting chiefs heard Jean duSable's same powerful and convincing plea for peace as the earlier council had. This time acceptance was quick. The leaders of the southern tribes praised the dead Pontiac, the noble chief who so often scourged them, for calling for an end to Indian wars on the Great Lakes.

"The wisdom of the Great Spirit surely fell upon the Great Pontiac in his final hour," one Miami said.

"In the end he thought only of his Indian brethren," said an Illinois.

This chief even promised to find the brave who had assassinated Pontiac and bring him to justice, though it was likely the dishonorable murderer was already hidden behind the protective walls of some British fort.

It took several days to work out details of the treaty:

No hunting parties would infringe on the lands of the Ottawas or Potawatomis without permission, nor their hunting parties on the lands of the Illinois and Miami. No raiding parties would henceforth steal livestock, oxen or food from each other. No Indian bands would attack any villages under the protection of the four Indian nations. No Indian braves would carry off squaws, children, or other prisoners to make them wives or slaves. And the nations agreed to immediately release all slaves now held in custody allowing them, if they chose, to return to their native villages. The prisoner exchange would not include captive squaws taken as wives.

If an Indian or group of Indians violated any of these agreements the violators would be brought to immediate justice.

The four nations, in working out territorial claims, agreed that the Mississippi, Illinois, Ohio, and Maumee rivers would be declared open waters by treaty now, rather than by simple tradition. They also agreed to allow Indian traders or trappers to travel unmolested over the various beaten trails of the Midwest.

The Ottawas, most powerful of the four nations, did not let the Miami and Illinois off without land concessions. The Ottawas demanded no territorial gains for themselves but insisted that certain lands of northern Illinois, Indiana and Ohio be ceded to the Potawatomis so that a neutral buffer zone would separate Ottawa country from Illinois and Miami country. The Ottawas suspected the British, their arch enemy, might at some future time incite Miami or Illinois tribes. Any such attacks would now have to cross the Potawatomi Buffer, giving the Ottawas a readymade ally. The Potawatomis tempered these terms, however, by giving Miami and Illinois Indians travel rights over all trails and rivers leading to any of the Great Lakes.

Among the lands given to the Potawatomis was the centuries-old battleground of Eschikagou. If all nations abided by the treaty, no war parties would ever again clash in battle on the pink, flowered plains.

Jean duSable felt pride in the treaty. He had brought peace where few men now living had ever known peace before. Furthermore, he had carried out the last wishes of the great Pontiac, an accomplishment that truly entitled him to wear the honor belt girding his waist. Finally, the prospect of building a cabin at Eschikagou, and even opening a trading post there, brightened.

By midsummer of 1769 the various chiefs of the four midwestern nations completed consultations with the elders and subchiefs of various tribes. Sparks of opposition arose here or there but no one seriously challenged the peace treaty. In a final parley and celebration at St. Joseph, forty-six chiefs and subchiefs, including Pokagon, formally agreed to the treaty. Peace had come to the Great Lakes for the first time in over a half century. Only the British were disappointed.

Jean duSable now found himself torn. He liked the Eschikagou plain and there was little doubt that Pokagon would allow him to build there, yet he did not really want to live among the Indians. He missed Jacques Clemorgan, but he disliked dealing with Spaniards. Only two months ago it had been Chief Pokagon who struggled with a hard decision, now it was Jean wrestling.

"All of us honor you, Jean duSable," Pokagon said. "You have done the impossible and won the heart of every Great Lakes Indian. For our part, you are welcome to stay among us forever, but I know that you long for your trading post and your dear friend in St. Louis. So, you must do what you think is best for yourself."

Jean might have decided to return to St. Louis and Jacques Clemorgan except for a new element entering his life at St. Joseph. He had first met Catherine, beautiful cousin of Pokagon, in the old mission church where he had gone to pray and where she, too, knelt. Her Christian name was inherited from an ancient ancestor who had been baptized by one of the now legendary Black Robes. Almost from the start Jean was certain he had fallen in love with her. He liked her long shiny hair, her big, sparkling brown eyes, her smooth clean face. She talked softly and always with a deep respect for the

Haitian. The pretty Potawatomi princess had returned Jean's initial look of admiration and before long was cooking for him, washing his clothing, or cleaning the small visitor's lodge. They took long walks together over the valley and through the forest and paddled a canoe on the St. Joseph River, sharing a concern for nature's creations. She loved the birds, the woods, the clear brooks, the animals of the forest, and the multicolored wild flowers of Michigan.

"The pink-stemmed flowers of the Eschikagou plain are most beautiful," Jean once told the girl.

"So I am told," Catherine answered him softly. "Perhaps you may someday take me there so that we can walk among the Eschikagou flowers together."

"Perhaps."

Neither Chief Pokagon nor Catherine's parents objected to their close relationship but appeared as delighted as the other Indians in St. Joseph. In a letter sent to Clemorgan by runner, Jean wrote of the beautiful Catherine and his strong attachment.

In his reply, Jacques told him: "Marry her! She is what you need. All men should have a wife."

This encouragement erased any remaining doubts. Jean was certain that the pretty girl loved him as much as he loved her. When he spoke to Chief Pokagon the young chief smiled and placed a hand on his shoulder.

"I could not be more pleased than to see my cousin become your wife. But even Potawatomi chiefs are not all powerful. It is our law that you must seek the permission of the squaw's parents."

They welcomed him with smiles until he asked permission to take Catherine as his bride. Then the girl's parents suddenly became somber.

"Jean duSable, cherished friend of the Potawatomis," Catherine's father said, "much as we would like to see our daughter become your bride, this cannot be. Although some of our people do intermarry with non-Potawatomis, we hold to the old laws—that none can marry outside of the tribe. I

52

am sorry, good friend. We cannot allow Catherine to marry a white man."

"W-white man!" Jean cried. "I'm no white man."

"Nor are you a Potawatomi."

Jean's heart sank. Suddenly he forgot all his accomplishments on the Great Lakes, forgot about Pokagon, the peace treaty, even the Eschikagou plain. His mind reeled from disappointment. So shocked was he by the refusal that he made no attempt to change the minds of the girl's parents. He went dejectedly to Pokagon and told him that he was returning at once to St. Louis.

Pokagon, seeing no reason to ask why when the answer was already etched on Jean's face, simply pressed Jean's wrist in sympathy. "May the Great Spirit go with you."

So, three months after he first saw the Eschikagou plain, Jean duSable crossed it again on his way back to St. Louis. He paid no attention to the wide colorful fields; nor did he look at the game-filled streams and the dense rich forests in the distance. The shock of losing Catherine had shattered his dreams of settling on this fabulous portage connecting the great inland waterway of the continent. He wanted only to get away from the Great Lakes. Even though now open to settlement Eschikagou would remain an uncultivated paradise for the time being.

With each passing week of Jean's absence Jacques Clemorgan had become more worried, fearing he might never again see his boyhood friend, so he gratefully welcomed his return. The white man tried to comfort his friend in his loss of Catherine, suggesting a New Orleans vacation or a visit home for a reunion with their fathers. After all, they did run a successful business, had amassed considerable money, and could afford the trip to the Caribbean.

But nothing Jacques did or suggested could raise Jean's spirits. He simply wanted to get away. He decided to take a winter trek up the Missouri River wilderness to gather furs. Jacques did not discourage him but insisted that he take along a companion. Choctaw had not returned to St. Louis

53

with Jean, but there was a host of Indians around St. Louis eager for the chance.

By spring, when he returned to St. Louis with two bundles of pelts, Jean had overcome some of his disappointment. Jacques had bought some good furs himself during the winter so they had a good stock to sell in New Orleans and he persuaded Jean to close up the trading post for the summer and accompany him. They would enjoy a comfortable vacation in the gulf city, then sail on to Haiti for a month's visit.

"We've worked too hard for the past several years," Jacques told his partner. "We deserve a few months away from business."

The trip south took Jean duSable far from the Great Lakes and Catherine but he had not forgotten either. He did not enjoy the luxuries of fine restaurant food, comfortable hotel beds, or the gay night life of New Orleans; only his visit to Father Gibault brought a measure of comfort.

"My son," Father Gibault told the Haitian, "God has already worked miracles through you. Sometimes we're not put on this earth to win gains for ourselves but to bring good to others. Your heart aches for this Indian girl, but think of the great joy you have brought to thousands of God's children on their lands in the Great Lakes. They may now live in peace and security because you taught them the way of peace. Think, too, how you have shared with God the fruits of your own hard labor by aiding our mission. Your generosity has enabled us to help many ill-clothed and hungry people.

"Do not grieve for yourself or become bitter because God does not reward you on this earth. Think of the good He has done for so many through you. And after all, my son, what is this life but a preparation for the eternal life? As for us at the mission, we shall always remember you in our prayers and thank God that He sent you to New France."

As the two young Haitians prepared for their trip home, a new blow came. Before even buying their sailing ship tickets a letter arrived from San Marc saying Jean's father had died. He could not bear the thought of returning without his father there. So Jacques went to Haiti alone. Jean remained with Father Gibault for the summer, losing himself in helping others and soon finding enough satisfaction in it to forget his own sorrows.

Back in St. Louis in the fall of 1770, Jean and Jacques worked busily to reopen their trading post, Jean himself planning eagerly for a new expedition up the Missouri. The two partners got a pleasant surprise—a visit from Choctaw. He brought with him a bundle of otter pelts, the richest that they had ever seen. Where had he got them?

"Eschikagou," Choctaw said. "Since the treaty, we are able to trap on the great portage in peace and safety."

"Jean," Jacques said, "these pelts are unbelievable. They gleam like sheets of gold. The furs are as thick as cotton rolls, and the texture as soft as delicate velvet. Perhaps you should make your winter trek to this portage of which Choctaw speaks instead of going up the Missouri."

"I will gladly take you with me," Choctaw said.

"I'm sure Choctaw can guide you," Jacques told his partner.

"I know the way to Eschikagou," Jean said, somewhat piqued, the sudden memory of Des Plaines bringing back a tinge of bitterness. He looked at Choctaw. "We will leave at once for a winter on the Great Lakes."

They set out in a dugout canoe, carrying axes, a saw, guns, several blankets, and other necessities for a long winter stay. While they traveled northward Choctaw suggested they build a cabin on the Illinois River since the bitter winds of Lake Michigan sliced across Des Plaines like sharp knives during the winter. They could make trips to Eschikagou, set traps, and then return to the milder Illinois River.

As they approached the Great Lakes region Jean thought again of St. Joseph and the beautiful Catherine. He questioned Choctaw. All was well in St. Joseph, Choctaw told him. Pokagon ruled fairly and honestly. His subjects liked him. The Potawatomis devoted most of their time and energy to farming, livestock, hunting, fishing, and building new lodges, things now possible because they found no need to spend themselves in war or war preparations. The tribe seemed happy and contented. If they had felt any disappointment because they had not gone to war over Pontiac's murder, there was no evidence of it now in the St. Joseph valley.

While Jean appreciated hearing this current news about the Potawatomis he was more anxious for news of Catherine. He finally asked. Choctaw told him that the pretty Catherine was in good health but that she no longer smiled. Like any obedient daughter she had accepted the decision of her parents. She had not, however, concerned herself with seeking a husband nor had her parents attempted to force her.

Jean listened, both satisfied and hurt, glad the girl still thought about him, sorry she was unhappy. Why not pay a visit to St. Joseph Choctaw suggested. Not only Pokagon and Catherine, but many other Indians there would be delighted to see him again. Jean promised to consider such a visit but made no commitment.

Within a few days he and Choctaw had built a rude cabin on the Illinois River, thirty miles below the Eschikagou plain, and chopped and stacked a full cord of firewood for the winter. Then they took trips northward to set traps on Des Plaines River. Jean did not mind the winter wind from Lake Michigan or the heavy snows; the crisp cold climate only encouraged him to work harder. And the cold made doubly comfortable the warmth of his snug cabin on the Illinois River.

Several times during the winter Choctaw offered to watch the traps himself if Jean wanted to visit St. Joseph. Three times small groups of Potawatomi hunters visited Eschikagou and offered to take him back with them to St. Joseph. Still Jean refused. He lacked the courage to face Catherine again, knowing he could not have her as his bride.

After three months on the Great Lakes bundles of rich otter pelts had been gathered. In March, when the ice broke up on Des Plaines and Illinois rivers, Jean and Choctaw loaded their canoe, boarded up their cabin, and started southward to St. Louis.

"You will do well with these pelts," Choctaw told Jean. "We can return again next fall and bring more traps with us to gather even more."

That spring's trip south with Jacques Clemorgan to sell their pelts in New Orleans found astonished buyers ogling the rich otter furs and paying handsome prices for them. Somehow Jean felt no satisfaction in their admiration, nor did he enjoy the comforts and gaieties of New Orleans any more this time than last. Again his only comfort came from Father Gibault.

The following winter, 1772, when Choctaw and Jean returned to the Great Lakes area for another winter of trapping, Jean insisted on building a cabin on the Eschikagou plain itself, despite the cold. He constructed it on the Chicago River, right on the heart of the portage between Lake Michigan and Des Plaines. From here, he and Choctaw could not only set traps to the south but also to the north where otters wore even thicker furs.

In February, while Jean and Choctaw were in their cabin drying out furs, they received a surprise visitor—Pokagon. Jean and the young chief embraced with fervor.

"Honored friend," Pokagon said, "you are welcome to the lands of the Potawatomis."

"Yes, Eschikagou does belong to the Potawatomis," Jean said.

"But," Pokagon said, "except for a few of our people who do some hunting and fishing here, we have not made use of these lands."

"How did you know I was here?"

"Every Indian on the Great Lakes knows that the dark-skinned peacemaker traps at Eschikagou," Pokagon replied.

Jean smiled. "I suppose I must apologize. I have built a cabin here and set traps here. I am a trespasser and perhaps I deserve punishment. I should have sought your permission."

"Yes," Pokagon said amiably. "This is your second winter here but I am disappointed because you have not come to see us on the St. Joseph. Catherine too is disappointed. She misses you, just as I hope you long to see her. So, I have come myself to ask you to visit us."

"To face Catherine again," Jean said, "would be like seeing a beautiful flower that one cannot touch."

Pokagon squeezed Jean's wrist—he should definitely visit St. Joseph, he would not be disappointed, he grinned. Not only did Catherine want to see him, but her parents also.

"Her parents?" Jean asked in surprise.

"Come, dear friend," Pokagon pleaded.

Jean duSable could hardly decline the invitation after Pokagon had come all this way to Eschikagou. Choctaw, as he had the year before, offered to care for the cabin, traps, and pelts; Pokagon left two Indians at Eschikagou to help.

Within a week the villagers at St. Joseph were greeting the great peacemaker with warm handgrips and friendly cries. Jean wasted no time in visiting Catherine's parents. He saw her looking as beautiful as ever, and his heart pumped furiously, his nerves tingled. No man was more in love than Jean duSable.

"Honored one," Catherine's father asked him, "do you still desire my daughter as wife?"

Jean replied, "More than life itself but not against the wishes of her parents." Catherine's father nodded gratefully. The girl's spirits had been drained out of her, he said, ever since Jean left St. Joseph. He and his wife had tried vigorously to reawaken her vibrant eagerness for life, always before evident in their daughter, but she had lost all ambition and interest. Her thoughts were only of Jean. They had heard that he too had brooded for months. Perhaps the Great Spirit willed the union. At any rate, they were now willing to give him Catherine if he still desired to marry her.

Jean duSable, greatly tempted, slowly shook his head. He was unwilling to violate Potawatomi law even for Catherine.

Her father placed a hand on Jean's shoulder, saying there

was a way, and without breaking Potawatomi law. He had already counseled with Pokagon and the medicine men. The Potawatomi tribe could adopt Jean and make him one of them. Would he consent to this adoption?

Jean eagerly agreed.

Catherine's father raised his hands and smiled. They would carry out the adoption ceremony at once and prepare a marriage feast. And the Potawatomis would also prepare a lodge where the couple could live as man and wife.

"You will have no need to build us a lodge," Jean told Catherine's father. "We already have one."

"You have one?"

"Yes," Jean answered, "at Eschikagou."

Chapter Seven

Spring had once again come to the Eschikagou plain when two canoes thudded against the western shoreline. The breeze from Lake Michigan sent a comfortable whisk across the portage, the sun beamed a pleasant warmth on the plains where the buds of countless pink-flowered plants had burst into bloom and the dormant grasses greened.

Catherine was a princess and, in the custom of the Potawatomis, Chief Pokagon had sent four Indians along to help her establish her new home in Eschikagou, and work for Jean du-Sable if Catherine so desired. The four began their service by unloading blankets, clothing, cooking utensils, pottery, food, and other items from the canoe while Jean duSable gazed eagerly about the plains. Not only could he build at Eschikagou but he had Catherine to share the adventure with him.

They moved in leisurely manner through the flower-strewn fields. There was only a rude cabin here now, Jean said excitedly, putting words to his dream, but in time he would change the uninhabited plain into a settlement as busy and active as St. Joseph. He would build her a mansion house, a home surpassing anything ever seen in the Great Lakes country. He would cultivate acres of corn, wheat, squash, and other crops, raise swaying fields of alfalfa for his herds of grazing livestock and build dairy barns, milk houses, smokehouses. Finally, he would erect a trading post and a lodging house for the comfort of travelers using this portage. Yes, Jean nodded half to himself and half to Catherine, Eschikagou would become greater than St. Joseph, perhaps even greater than Detroit or St. Louis.

She merely smiled in tender amusement. Her beloved's head was filled with ambitious dreams. If they spent a lifetime in the cabin she would be content to serve him faithfully as dutiful wife. On this first day at Eschikagou they spent the night in the shelter built during the past winter's trapping season. She gathered firewood and cooked their evening meal outdoors in the chill evening, and found only a bundle of otter furs to sleep upon, but she happily accepted these discomforts. The Indian servants struck teepees nearby for their own quarters.

The sun broke warm and clear the following morning. Jean duSable awoke restless with eagerness and, as Catherine prepared breakfast, he brought the four Indians together.

"We cannot have a Potawatomi princess living in such a rude cabin," he told them. "Our first task will be to build a house for her." Jean pointed to the dense pine forests a league to the north.

For the next several weeks he, obsessed, and the four Indians, even Catherine, toiled from dawn to dusk. They hewed sturdy pines, trimmed off branches, then dragged the logs for three miles over the plains to a marked site on the Eschikagou River. Large stones were lifted from the shoreline of Lake Michigan, and slate to build the floor, roof and chimney. There would be no open holes in his house but a real fireplace with outside chimney. The sturdy slate could withstand the heaviest snow or the most driving rain.

The finished structure, four rooms deep, measured eighteen feet in width and forty feet in length. Besides a parlor with a huge stone fireplace Jean built one room as a kitchen with a smaller fireplace for cooking and laid out two sleeping rooms. Each room contained at least one window covered with tanned deerskin to keep out the cold at night but which could be rolled up for light during the day. There were three doors, two at the rear of the house and one at the front.

The slate floor was laid throughout the four rooms to keep out mud and dust he covered with bearskin rugs to keep the surface warm. From smaller logs he built chairs, tables, shelves, and beds, covering the beds with tough deerskin and setting two blankets on each. Finally, the Indians cleared away the brush from in front of the house so that Catherine and Jean could plant a flower garden.

By the end of June the house was completed. Catherine could only stare in astonishment for, with the help of the Indians, duSable had built the most elaborate cabin home ever seen in the Great Lakes area. She had never expected such a large and luxurious house; Jean had made no idle boast when they came here in late April. And, even before finishing the house he had cleared two acres of land and planted corn, wheat and squash. They would have plenty of stored food next winter.

"Catherine," Jean said to her one early July day, "we have worked hard since coming to Eschikagou and deserve a change. I should go back to St. Louis to see to our business. Would you like to visit my dear friend, Jacques Clemorgan?"

"I will go wherever my husband asks."

"Perhaps you would prefer to spend a few weeks in St. Joseph."

"If it is your desire to visit St. Louis, then it is also my desire."

Jean duSable left the four Indians to care for the newly planted crops at Eschikagou, instructing them to keep the rows of plants free from weeds and bugs, to harvest the squash and corn when they ripened and store the harvest in a teepee.

Jean and Catherine launched their canoe on the other side

of the portage on Des Plaines River, carrying with them only some food, clothing, and a few gifts for Jacques Clemorgan. Catherine, quiet and reserved, said very little during the trip downriver, most of the time smiling and listening to the Haitian as he spoke of his friendship with Clemorgan: how they had grown up together in the Caribbean, suffered dangers together and built a successful business together.

In St. Louis a happy Jacques met Jean with an affectionate hug and kisses on both cheeks, Catherine was pleased to be a quiet witness. Such friendships were not common around the Great Lakes area.

Jacques finally looked at the pretty Indian and a smile lit up his face as he took her hand, patted it gently, then kissed her softly on the cheek. "You're as beautiful as any woman I've ever seen," he said. "Now I understand why Jean brooded over you for two years." Catherine lowered her head modestly. "Whatever is here, whatever we have, they are as much yours as they are mine and Jean's. Welcome to St. Louis, Catherine."

For the next two days Jean and Catherine enjoyed the frontier comforts of St. Louis. They sat in soft chairs as they talked and slept in comfortable beds that Jacques said he had imported from New Orleans, hoping Jean didn't mind. When they did not eat at home Jacques took them to dine in one of the two inns now in St. Louis.

He reported that the trading post had done well this past year, several barges of furs having been sold in New Orleans, the pelts sent down from Eschikagou bringing especially good prices. Their partnership was in good financial condition with over ten thousand livres at the Banco de Orleans.

Jean, though pleased with Jacques' financial report, seemed more excited about Eschikagou. He told Clemorgan of the mansion house just completed on the plains, of the crops planted, of the good trapping on the portage. The more Jean rambled the more uneasy Jacques felt. Jean spoke too lovingly of this Eschikagou and apparently meant to live there permanently. The idea disturbed Clemorgan who had grown fond of the St. Louis fur trade center and his regular trips to New Orleans.

When his partner frowned, Jean smiled. "Do not be upset because I have now come to love Eschikagou as you love St. Louis. Is that so bad? We can still do business together."

"If it be God's will," the white man answered.

Jean had a proposition. Why must they operate a single business place? Since they had considerable money perhaps Jacques would agree to invest some of it in a second business at Eschikagou. They could build a trading post and a lodging house there and Clemorgan still place the wholesale orders in New Orleans, only buy more for transportation to both St. Louis and Eschikagou—everything from jars of molasses to coffee, from simple knives to pirogues. Right in the middle of the North American wilderness, on the great portage linking the Atlantic Ocean and the Gulf of Mexico, the Eschikagou trading post and lodging house would become the oasis of the interior continent!

"Think of it, Jacques, think of it" Jean said excitedly, beaming with anticipation. "We would have a trading post on the legendary plains of LaSalle. We would fulfill an ambition as old as French America itself."

Clemorgan shook his head in a mixture of admiration and amusement. Jean duSable loved that wild Great Lakes portage as much as life itself. Jacques had not seen his friend so excited or so eager since that day they had left New Orleans with Choctaw on their first venture into the interior wilderness.

"I have found the place that only exists in good men's dreams," Jean continued. "We have ended the Indian wars and the plains are now safe. Once travelers learn they can cross this portage without fear or hardship our business will grow at Eschikagou."

Clemorgan did not answer.

"Would it be so terrible if we owned two trading posts?" Jean asked again. "Would it, Jacques? You care for the business in St. Louis, I for the new business on the Great Lakes?"

64

Clemorgan nodded in agreement. He suggested an immediate trip to New Orleans to buy whatever merchandise, equipment and supplies needed to build and stock at Eschikagou. But Jean asked his partner to make these purchases himself and bring them to Des Plaines. After all, Jacques knew much more about stocking a trading post than he did. He himself would return to Eschikagou and begin construction of a trading post and lodging house so that the buildings would be completed before the first snows or before Jacques brought in merchandise and supplies. Jean said he would take with him from the St. Louis trading post some emergency necessities—two oxen, a plow, some tools, a crosscut saw, some lengths of chain, and a couple of oil lamps, if agreeable—and promised to send Choctaw to St. Louis as Jacques' guide to the Eschikagou portage. Clemorgan nodded, but expressed sorrow that Jean and Catherine were not to spend more time in St. Louis, perhaps even take a vacation trip to New Orleans.

"Be patient," Jean answered, "for the time is not far off when we will spend much time together, just as we did long ago."

Jacques Clemorgan nodded again hiding the sadness he felt, fearing their days of close companionship were over. He was facing up to a hard truth that as yet Jean had not: Jacques still belonged to the white man's culture and Jean, a black man who had been raised in that culture, was now joining the Indian culture—two different worlds.

By the end of August 1772, Jean Baptiste Pointe duSable and his wife were back in their new mansion house at Eschikagou. In their absence, the Indian servants had brought other Indians from the St. Joseph to help with the harvest and the building of a bark storage barn.

Jean was delighted with the healthy first harvest, but he spent little time in congratulating himself. He sent a runner to St. Joseph to summon Choctaw and then set about building a lodging house and trading post, the two strong oxen, the saw, and the heavy chain greatly reducing the work of cutting and hauling logs from the forest. Jean devised two chain assemblies, hitched one to each oxen, and set two Indians to hewing trees, some others to dragging the timber from the forest to the place where he and others cut it into measured lengths.

For the trading post Jean built an oblong of logs about a hundred yards below the mansion house on the Eschikagou river. In it he laid a hard clay floor, covered with sand to keep it soft and dry, and cut four windows, a front door, and a rear door. Then he constructed a counter and hung the walls with shelves made of split logs. As with the mansion house, there was also a fireplace to keep the trading post warm during the winter. Because of having more tools he finished the building in half the time needed to construct the mansion house.

By the end of September, as he was preparing to start building the lodging house, Choctaw arrived at Eschikagou, so Jean took a two day rest to enjoy a pleasant visit with his Indian friend before sending him to St. Louis to await Jacques Clemorgan.

Jean designed the lodging house in a square, divided into seven rooms, two at the rear, two at each side and in the center facing the front a large room for use as a comfortable guest parlor and dining area. In this large center room he built a stone fireplace with an outside chimney.

"Visitors will find warmth and comfort here even on the coldest winter day," he told Catherine.

The walls of this building were of peeled upright logs, coated with creosote to keep them weatherproof, cross-beamed under another slate roof. Dried deerskin was hung over each window in the sleeping rooms and in the front sanded-floor parlor for which he constructed birch furniture. To finish off the six sleeping rooms he built log beds, two to each of four rooms, covering them with tanned hides and two blankets. In the other two he merely put buffalo or bear-skin rugs on the floor, since these two rooms would be reserved for Indian visitors who preferred not to sleep on the elevated cots of the white man.

Over the front door of both his trading post and lodging house Jean put up the same kind of signs: BIEN-VENUE À DES PLAINES (Welcome to Des Plaines). And above the signs he painted on a bark plaque the picture of an elk, symbol of the Potawatomis who owned Eschikagou. He was, after all, an adopted Potawatomi.

By the time Jean duSable had finished these two structures at the end of October, he and Catherine and the Indian servants had consumed enough of their harvest to leave room in the storage barns for two stalls for his oxen.

About a week later two French trappers arrived at Eschikagou from Quebec. They gaped in astonishment at the cultivated ground and the sturdy buildings on Des Plaines.

They had come this way, they said, after hearing about some kind of Indian truce on the portage and been further encouraged at St. Joseph by Chief Pokagon who told them that a Frenchman, a black, had helped bring about this peace. However, they had only hoped to find safety at Eschikagou, not an oasis in the wilderness. The trip from Quebec had been harsh, with only a few Indian villages or small settlements between the St. Lawrence River and the Great Lakes. The trappers, hardly able to believe this comfortable way station existed at the halfway point between the Great Lakes and the Mississippi, willingly paid Jean for bed and board at the lodging house.

Jean apologized to them for the empty shelves in the trading post and the lack of transportation between the shores of Lake Michigan and Des Plaines River, a distance of three leagues (nine miles), but promised by next spring to have a full stock of supplies in his trading post and a road cut between Lake Michigan and Des Plaines. There would be oxen and wagon team to portage travelers, their baggage and their canoes across the plains in comfort.

The two trappers told Jean that he had already transformed a bleak wilderness into a place of convenience, for which they expressed gratitude and wished the Negro luck. After a two-day stay they launched their canoe in Des Plaines River to continue their journey southward, promising to tell everyone they met of the great change and the fine hospitality that had come to Des Plaines.

Several days after the trappers left Jacques Clemorgan finally reached Eschikagou. Jean's first hint of his arrival came when Choctaw emerged from the west.

"Bring your oxen and travois at once to Des Plaines River. Your partner waits for you there."

Within a half hour Jean was eagerly leading his teams across the plain. When he reached the river he gaped. Jacques Clemorgan had tied an entire flotilla of boats—six of them—against the shoreline, the pirogues manned by a dozen Indians.

"Well, Jean, don't just stand there," he grinned. "Get these boats unloaded."

However, Jean duSable continued to stare at the loaded pirogues, for it appeared that Jacques Clemorgan had brought half of New Orleans with him: four oxen, two plows, a half dozen bit saws for cutting timber, shot, lead bullets, powder horns, and dozens of blankets; several kegs of coffee, bags of sugar, salt, and spices; crates of molasses, and tins of tobacco. One pirogue alone was packed with boots, coats, hats, cooking and eating utensils, jars, and casks to store food. Another contained wheels, axles, chains, leather thongs, an anvil, tongs, sledge hammers, and other items to equip a blacksmith shop.

Even with available help Jean and Jacques needed two days to transport the mass of equipment, food, and merchandise from the Des Plaines River to the trading post. There the mounds of supplies filled every shelf in the building and spilled over into the small storeroom at the rear. Jacques had also brought ledgers, quilled pens and ink for Jean to keep a record of his accounts.

When they had finally completed the work Jacques gave Jean and Catherine some special house gifts bought in New Orleans: a set of china and copper kettles, linen and pillows, a set of books for Jean because he loved to read, several oil lamps, and finally two silk dresses for Catherine. She stared in fascination, fingering the delicate cloth in awe.

"Our thanks, dear friend," Jean said to Clemorgan.

"You and Catherine deserve more."

"You'll be a first guest in our house."

For the next several days Clemorgan simply enjoyed the hospitality of Eschikagou. Jean and Jacques ate heartily, slept soundly at night and spent many days walking together about the Eschikagou plain. Jean showed his friend where to set traps on Des Plaines and Eschikagou rivers and where he had planted crops and hoped to clear more land, enough in time for livestock.

Finally, the two men turned to business. Clemorgan explained that he had spent nearly 2,500 livres to buy and transport all these things to Eschikagou. But, besides the stocked trading post in St. Louis, Clemorgan and duSable still had 8,000 livres at the Banco de Orleans.

"Fine," Jean said, "we can keep our trading posts well stocked."

"No," Clemorgan said solemnly. "Jean, dear friend to whom I owe my life and my fortune, I fear we must dissolve our partnership."

Jean's mind reeled, his face frozen in shock, and he blinked in disbelief.

Clemorgan put a hand on Jean's shoulder and then led him over the Eschikagou plain. "It is for the best," he said.

They had been drifting in separate directions for the past three years or more, he said, ever since Jean had left the bedside of the dying Pontiac to visit St. Joseph and find two new loves. His whole body, mind and soul now belonged to the beautiful Catherine and the Eschikagou plain. Neither man could deny this change. Clemorgan, too, had found new interests during these years, new friends in New Orleans and St. Louis, and yes, some of them were Spaniards; he hoped Jean would forgive him for this.

He suggested that they divide their wealth, four thousand livres for Jean and four thousand for Jacques, Jean to keep everything here at Eschikagou and Jacques the trading post in St. Louis. If desired, Jacques would turn over to Jean half of the buyer accounts they had in New Orleans. Any half he wanted.

Jean shook his head vigorously. His heart had grown heavier as Jacques talked on. He wanted to lash out angrily at his white partner, accuse him of breaking their lifelong friendship, but no words came because inside he also knew that Jacques was right. It was suddenly clear that he was indeed in a new world, a world at the other end of the Mississippi River, a life far from the crowded gaiety of New Orleans or bustling St. Louis. He belonged no more to the South; not to St. Louis or New Orleans, not even to Haiti. For better or for worse his future lay in the Great Lakes country.

When finally he could manage an answer, he agreed to end their long and happy partnership. And how did Jean want his share of the eight thousand livres? He shrugged, but Jacques told him it would be unwise to keep that much cash around his house or his trading post. Should the money be left in the Banco de Orleans? Jean thought for a moment and then stared at the wide expanse of Lake Michigan to the east. He belonged to the Great Lakes and the east.

"Transfer my share to the Bank of Quebec," he said.

With this heavy problem settled, Jean Baptiste Pointe du-Sable and Jacques Clemorgan reverted once more to leisure. For another week they enjoyed hunting, trapping and fishing around Lake Michigan just as they had many years ago on the shores and waters of the Caribbean.

Finally, the time came for departure. Jean and Jacques bade each other farewell on the banks of Des Plaines River, hugging each other for a full minute, promising to see each other as often as possible—Clemorgan visiting Eschikagou and Jean visiting St. Louis.

As the pirogue moved downstream Jean, on the bank, peered hard as it faded in the distance. Clemorgan, too, squinted back at the lonely figure for a last glimpse, finally turning and digging his paddle into the river.

Jean sighed when he started back across the Eschikagou plain. Deep in their hearts what both men feared was that this meeting might be their last.

Chapter Eight

The two French trappers who had stopped at the lodging house in October must have quickly spread the word that Eschikagou had become a haven in the wilderness. During the winter of 1772–73 eighteen Quebec-bound wayfarers stopped at the portage on the way east from the upper Mississippi valley. In Canada, these new visitors continued to spread the word. By late winter not only trappers but roving frontiersmen and traveling merchants had also stopped at Eschikagou to enjoy the comforts of the lodging house.

Jean Baptiste Pointe duSable, recognizing the growing importance of the Eschikagou portage, spent most of the winter in planning to expand. He picked out sites on which to construct other buildings. He set aside tracts of land for alfalfa fields and pastures. He laid out a route for a road across the plains from the shores of Lake Michigan to the banks of Des Plaines River.

He also spent many hours talking to these winter visitors, especially those from Quebec. What kind of goods and services were available in the east? Could these supplies be delivered to Eschikagou? Could cattle dealers transport livestock to these plains? How about seed for planting crops and fruit trees? What about hardware—harness, chains, wagon wheels, springs, and so forth?

For answer most of the guests at the lodging house pointed to Detroit, 275 miles to the east. This largest settlement west of the Appalachian Mountains included two wholesale and several retail merchants. Further east one could buy more goods at Fort Niagara on Lake Ontario, or purchase anything one wanted at Montreal on the St. Lawrence River. Best of all, the prices for goods and supplies in the province of Quebec were considerably less than the prices in New Orleans or St. Louis.

Most of the visitors also agreed that Jean should expand his services on Des Plaines, pointing out that the river port of St. Louis had grown steadily as an important fur trade center and, since it lay north of the Ohio River, the Great Lakes-Mississippi route became more desirable for trade than the Ohio valley route. Furthermore, from Quebec it was shorter, more direct, making the Eschikagou portage at the halfway point an ideal place to stop for rest and supplies.

In March of 1773 Catherine bore her first child, a son. The proud Jean duSable beamed happily but recognized the added responsibility to provide the best comfort and security he could for his wife and new son. So as soon as the Lake Michigan ice broke in April and the warm rays of the sun again penetrated the brisk lake air, he decided to make a trip eastward to find a wholesaler to supply his trading post and establish letters of credit at the Bank of Quebec. Two squaws came from St. Joseph to care for Catherine and her child during his absence.

With Choctaw and two other Indians Jean set out from the Eschikagou River in two canoes, carrying only simple necessities: food, coffee, blankets, guns, powder and balls, tobacco and cooking utensils. He stopped first at St. Joseph where Chief Pokagon welcomed him with a warm smile and a strong wrist grip. Jean spent two days here. As a result of the peace treaty, Pokagon said, the Potawatomis in the St. Joseph valley had continued to improve their lives, devoting their time to raising livestock, tilling land, and building strong lodges. Pokagon was glad to hear that Catherine and Jean's son enjoyed good health, and expressed satisfaction with the remarkable change that Jean had brought to Eschikagou. Travelers passing through St. Joseph had glowingly praised the hospitality they found on the portage.

Pokagon agreed with Jean's plans to expand Des Plaines settlement and wished him every success. Jean, in turn, suggested that the Potawatomis move to Eschikagou. The plains, vast and rich, offered room for lodges, planting corn, and raising livestock, the rich virgin soil being much better than the overworked soil of the St. Joseph valley.

Chief Pokagon stroked his chin. "Would you want others to infringe on the opportunities you have built for yourself at Eschikagou?"

"Honest men, willing to work, would not infringe on my labors," Jean said. "They would bring more growth to all."

The chief smiled. "You still think of others."

He promised to bring up the subject of moving Potawatomi families to Des Plaines at the next council meeting. Meanwhile, Pokagon wished Jean every success on his trip east but warned that Quebec and the lands to the east now belonged to the British and the British looked with suspicion upon men with French backgrounds.

After leaving the St. Joseph Jean and Choctaw and the other Indians continued their journey across the lower Michigan wilderness to Lake Erie, within several days reaching the busy settlement of Detroit. Here Jean for the first time saw British redcoats, off-duty soldiers from nearby Fort Detroit. He asked local residents about principal merchants, especially those who dealt in wholesale goods, and almost everyone in the settlement suggested Thomas Smith.

Smith met the Haitian with a warm handshake. The wholesaler knew of Jean's trading post at Eschikagou through several trappers' reports that more and more travelers had used

74

Des Plaines during the past winter. Detroit lay on the route from the St. Lawrence to Eschikagou so Thomas Smith was eager to sell merchandise to duSable.

Jean, remembering Pokagon's warning about the British, asked Smith about the redcoats. Would he suffer any difficulties with the British because of his French background, especially since he was black? Smith assured him the British never interfered with lawful merchants, and he offered to arrange a meeting with Colonel Arent Schuyler de Peyster who commanded the British troops at Fort Michilimackinac on Lake Huron. The colonel would be visiting Detroit in a few days.

Jean thanked Smith but he wanted to visit wholesalers in Fort Niagara, also the Bank of Quebec where funds had been transferred from the Banco de Orleans and where Jean's registered signature was required to establish letters of credit for any business dealings, including those with Thomas Smith. The Detroit wholesaler was delighted to hear about the letter of credit because hard money often fell into the hands of waylayers along the wilderness trail between Eschikagou and Detroit.

The two principal traders in the Fort Niagara settlement gave Jean a cool reception compared to the one received in Detroit. The name of Jean duSable and the Eschikagou portage had not as yet made an impact here but both wholesalers agreed to deal if Jean furnished a letter of credit from the Bank of Quebec. Somewhat deflated by their attitude, Jean decided to deal primarily with Thomas Smith. Besides, Fort Niagara lay too far east of Eschikagou, making the delivery of goods much longer. However, he might call on these Fort Niagara merchants if he could not get what he needed from Detroit, or if Thomas Smith tried to overcharge.

Not until May did Jean duSable and Choctaw arrive in Quebec, the largest town in French America outside of New Orleans. Crowds of people wove through the streets, dozens of busy shops lined the avenues, and sailing ships jammed the harbor, but the residents appeared more serious than those in

New Orleans and the city itself lacked the gulf port's air of gaiety and optimism. The British did not rule New Orleans as they now ruled Quebec.

French merchants and bankers still controlled the economy, however, so Jean was welcomed at the Bank of Quebec. He was a fellow Frenchman and, since slavery or prejudice was practically unheard of here Jean's black skin meant nothing.

"The funds from the Banco de Orleans arrived only recently," the bank manager said. "We had planned to send you a letter to this place called Eschikagou. How fortunate that you decided to personally visit us. Where is this Eschikagou?" He asked curiously. "And what do you do there?"

"The Eschikagou portage lies between the Great Lakes and the Mississippi River," Jean answered. "I have a trading post and lodging house there."

"Ah," the banker nodded. Then, checking Jean's signature with the signature from the Banco de Orleans, he nodded again in satisfaction. He would at once direct his clerk to write a letter of credit, and promised to accept no credit vouchers not bearing Jean duSable's signature. He hoped *Monsieur* would desposit future funds to his account here at the Bank of Quebec.

Jean spent a few days visiting some of the shops and inns with Choctaw, and before his departure, the heights of Quebec where the famous battle a decade ago had ended French rule in eastern North America. There on the battlefield he stared out at the mouth of the St. Lawrence River where it disappeared into the vast Atlantic Ocean, and was reminded of the mouth of another river—the Mississippi as it also disappeared into a vast sea—the Gulf of Mexico.

Suddenly a warm and excited feeling raced through his body. He, a Haitian, had now traveled the length of the inland waterway through the heart of the North American continent and was building at Eschikagou its crossroads between Quebec and New Orleans. For a moment Jean daydreamed. Perhaps the Eschikagou settlement on Des Plaines would one day become a city even more majestic and populous than either of these cities that anchored the great inland waterway.

A few weeks later, again arrived at Detroit, he once more called on Thomas Smith. The merchant's eyes gleamed when he saw the letter of credit and he said he hoped there would be a long and successful business relationship. Then he took Jean to Fort Detroit and introduced him to Colonel Arent Schuyler de Peyster, the British commander from Fort Michilimackinac.

The colonel, short and thin with a narrow face, appeared too small and too soft to command an army of soldiers in the tough wilderness of the Midwest. De Peyster smiled and gripped Jean's hand with surprising firmness.

"A pleasure to meet you, Mr. duSable," the colonel said. "I've heard great things about Des Plaines portage. I understand you've established a trading post and a comfortable inn for travelers. Such endeavors can only hasten the settlement of the Midwest. I wish you every success in your efforts."

"Thank you, Colonel," Jean answered. Ever wary of the British, he wondered if de Peyster really meant what he said. Colonel de Peyster caught the guarded look.

"You are unconvinced," the colonel grinned. "Be assured, Mr. duSable, neither I nor any other Britisher holds your French background against you. After all, most of the settlers in the Great Lakes area come from Louisiana or Quebec. They share the same French heritage as you do. They have simply become subjects of the British crown instead of the French crown. So long as they do not violate British laws, they will suffer no harm or harassment. We allow our subjects to move freely about the territories. Above all, you should know that, Mr. duSable," the colonel smiled, "I'm told that more and more visitors have crossed Des Plaines portage during this past year. So long as you continue to work and live peacefully there, as I understand you have, you will have no difficulties with the British crown."

"Eschikagou belongs to the Potawatomis," Jean said suddenly, irritated by the colonel's hint that the portage came under British jurisdiction.

77

"Perhaps," the officer answered. "In any event, have you been bothered by British soldiers?"

Jean admitted that he had seen none at Eschikagou; nor had anyone interfered with him.

"You've made a wise choice in your decision to deal with Thomas Smith," de Peyster said. "You'll find him honest and reliable."

"I'm sure I will."

Doubt still lingered in Jean's mind after the final friendly handshake. He felt that de Peyster *did* harbor a suspicion of him because of his French background. Worse, he did not like the inference that England had territorial claims to Eschikagou.

On Jean's return to St. Joseph, Chief Pokagon informed him the council had acted favorably on the suggestion that Potawatomi families move to Eschikagou, since the rich lands of the portage had been awarded to the Potawatomis at the peace council. Jean was delighted. Now Catherine would have some old St. Joseph neighbors to keep her company.

"We have spoken with the heads of households," Pokagon said, "and a hundred families have decided to move to Eschikagou."

"Will you be among them?" Jean asked.

"No," Pokagon answered, "my duty is here where I am close to the other Potawatomi tribes. But you will be. Families have been preparing to move for two or three weeks, waiting only for you to lead them to their new homes at Eschikagou."

Thus, on a warm morning in June, a procession of Potawatomi homesteaders filed out of St. Joseph to begin the journey over the trail around Lake Michigan instead of crossing it: old men, young men, old women, young women, and children of all ages and sizes. Oxen dragged travois loaded with household goods, food, and folded teepees. Pigs, cows, and even chickens straggled alongside.

Jean, anxious to return quickly to Eschikagou to begin construction of new buildings, felt that he could not leave the plodding immigrants behind when he himself had suggested the move. Fortunately a soothing warmth covered the Great Lakes, the weather was dry, the cavalcade moved west without difficulty over Indian trails, and found ample small game. During the evenings they sat around campfires—singing or telling legendary tales of great Potawatomi chieftains of the past—and slept under the stars in the cool comfortable night air.

After ten days they reached Eschikagou to be eagerly welcomed by the few Indians already living there, including Catherine. The heavy increase of inhabitants would end the loneliness on the vast portage.

As prescribed by Chief Pokagon and the St. Joseph council, each family could take one hundred acres of land on the plain, the chief having left the partitioning to leaders who had been in charge of the migrating families. Few squabbles arose and the newcomers were soon settled in temporary teepee shelters on their awarded tracts of land. Jean allowed them to use some of his tools to build permanent lodges on their new farms.

He himself immediately began construction of his own projects, devoting the rest of the summer to cutting a good road across the three leagues of plains between Lake Michigan and Des Plaines River. Oxen and plows leveled a roadbed, then oxen and wagons hauled tons of gravel to cover it, to keep the portage dry during spring and winter seasons. He also built two docks on the shore of Lake Michigan, and a smaller single dock on the banks of the river so that any traveler using the portage would know where to stop for transportation across the plains.

Two hired Indians maintained a constant vigil on these docks to greet visitors seeking passage, the Indians hurrying to the settlement for oxen and wagon, and carrying the traveler, his supplies and canoe over the plain on a road that skirted Jean's lodging house where wayfarers could rest for a day or two.

Over the next two years Jean continued to expand his Es-

79

chikagou enterprises. With the help of hired Indians from St. Joseph he worked hard during the warm months hauling logs from the forest and cutting them into planks with long cross-cut saws. Up went a dairy barn, a milk house, a horse mill (blacksmith shop), two cattle barns, a poultry house, a bake-shop, and finally a grist mill. The Indians gaped in amazement at this mill. Its bins held four or five times as much grain as did the Indian crushing bins made from pottery, and the grist itself swiftly and easily crushed corn or wheat into meal in a fraction of the time Indians could crush grain by hand.

The blacksmith shop clanged busily, shaping or repairing harnesses, wheels, axles, and horseshoes. Buildings like the bakeshop soon turned out loaves of hot bread by the dozens. And while the other buildings remained empty Jean promised livestock in the cattle barns, meat in the smokehouse, and cream in the milk house before another winter passed.

By October of 1775 several head of cattle and a large brood of chickens had arrived from Detroit, together with hay and bags of feed. The livestock housed in the barns and poultry house for the winter would be healthy and strong to reproduce the following spring.

"You have changed the face of Eschikagou," Choctaw told Jean.

"It is only the beginning," the Haitian answered. "Whatever conveniences we build here will encourage more people to use this portage. The trading post and the lodging house will grow in importance."

Now Jean concentrated on the land itself, along with Potawatomi Indians plowing acres of soil for fields of wheat, corn, hay, alfalfa and vegetable crops, and starting apple and peach orchards. His herds of dairy and beef cattle began supplying meat and dairy products in abundance and soon the Eschikagouans were exporting to Detroit beef, dairy foods, and vegetables.

More Potawatomi families moved into Eschikagou and following Jean's lead built their own poultry houses for their

80

own flocks of fowl. They took full advantage of Jean's grist mill which never stopped grinding cornmeal and flour, used the bakehouse that never grew cold for the hundreds of loaves of bread that daily came from its ovens. By the end of the year, the settlement's population had doubled.

Jean duSable built more docks on the shore of Lake Michigan not only to serve the almost daily arrival of travelers who crossed the portage but also the increasing commercial trade. Indians constantly loaded barges for eastward, or unloaded goods and supplies from Detroit, Fort Niagara, Fort Duquesne, or Quebec. Jean duSable's bank account fattened in Quebec.

Catherine meanwhile had delivered her second child in 1775, a daughter whom Jean called Suzanne after his mother. With a growing family, Jean now furnished his mansion house with more luxuries, importing real beds and upholstered furniture from Quebec, rich French walnut cabinets and dressers, loom-woven clothing for his wife and children, and for himself books.

By the summer of 1776 Jean was firmly established. Besides his commercial buildings, docks, and mansion house, most of the fruit orchards and livestock belonged to him.

"The settlement here now matches the settlement at St. Joseph," Choctaw told him.

"I tell you, Choctaw, I need no longer hope that Eschikagou will grow as large as St. Louis or Quebec. The time will come when Eschikagou will become the greatest city on this continent."

Jean duSable continued to dream the impossible dream. But, as Choctaw reflected and looked about Des Plaines community, a soberness came over him. The bleak uncivilized plain had blossomed into a thriving settlement. Even he could no longer doubt that Eschikagou would one day become a bustling city.

Chapter Nine

In the spring of 1777 the first impact of the Revolutionary War came to Eschikagou. Jean was leisurely strolling along the banks of Des Plaines River, watching his fishing poles in the water, when a canoe with a white man and an Indian at the paddles loomed from the south. Jean squinted downriver until it reached Des Plaines River dock and then, first gaping in astonishment, he chuckled delightedly. Jacques Clemorgan!

Within a few minutes he and his lifelong friend met on the river bank to hug each other fervently and then hop about the patch of ground like two elves in a fairytale ballet. Both the Indian in the canoe and the Indian on the dock stared at the two non-Indians acting like children, neither quite understanding the mutual love between the two men.

Jacques Clemorgan and Jean duSable, half skipping and half dancing, moved across the plain to the Eschikagou settlement. Indian farmers in the fields gazed in surprise at the strange behavior of the usually serious-minded Jean duSable. At the mansion house Catherine shared her husband's joy, willingly accepting Jacques' hug and kiss, a custom generally frowned upon by the Indian. She allowed Clemorgan to bounce on his knee the children who bawled in fright, unaccustomed as they were to this kind of juggling, especially from someone never seen before.

After Jacques enjoyed a fine dinner and a good pipe, the two men settled back in comfortable chairs.

"Unbelievable! Unbelievable!" Clemorgan said, staring about Jean's richly furnished mansion house. He studied the thick carpet, the rich drapes, the soft furniture on which they sat, and the sparkling cabinets of fine china. "You've done well for yourself, quite well."

"God has been good to us," Jean said.

"The change is remarkable," the white man said. He leaned forward and tapped Jean's arm. "I must confess that I doubted your dream, but you've made that dream come true. The wilderness has all but disappeared from these plains."

Jean thanked him. "And what of yourself, Jacques? How goes your trading post in St. Louis? And do you still enjoy your trips to the gay city of New Orleans?"

"Ah, Jean," his friend sighed, shaking his head. "Things have changed in these past few years. The Spanish and French in Louisiana resent each other more and more. The Spaniards want to rule the territory. The French, having lived in Louisiana for more than a century, are unwilling to give them total authority. So, the French protest, the Spaniards grow sterner. And now, because the British have turned their eyes to Louisiana, the Spaniards have tightened their rule. Things do not go well."

He went on to explain that Spain heavily taxed French merchants and now restricted their travel because of their growing discontent. The British on the other side of the Mississippi had been robbing honest French trappers and merchants seeking to escape the harsh Louisiana Spaniards of their goods, claiming that only Englishmen have any rights in British territory. Clemorgan's own business in the Mississippi valley had suffered badly because of high taxes, travel restrictions and stern rules on buying and selling though he had tried to make the best of a bad situation.

Jean expressed sympathy but the more Jacques talked the more Jean wondered. Clemorgan had not visited Jean in nearly three years. Why now?

"I am not here to seek your help, Jean," Jacques suddenly answered Jean's silent question, "though I know you would aid me if I asked." Then the white man looked soberly at the Negro. "I am leaving St. Louis and going to Virginia. I might lose my life in this choice so I wanted to visit you once more before I left."

Nonsense! Jean laughed. The Midwest, the Mississippi valley, the Ohio valley, the whole continent of North America was now at peace. Despite the harsh Spanish rule or British authority Clemorgan's life could certainly not be in danger. Why worry about a trip to Virginia?

But Jacques remained solemn. He intended to join the American colonists in their rebellion against England and take up arms.

"You mean fight?" Jean asked in surprise. "But this rebellion by a few English malcontents is no concern of yours."

"It is everyone's concern," Clemorgan answered. Didn't Jean himself condemn the harsh Spaniards and the authoritative British? Didn't he seek out Eschikagou as a place to escape their tyrannies? Didn't the Spanish kill Jean's mother, and the English Jean's good friend, Chief Pontiac?

The rebels numbered much more than a few malcontents, Clemorgan continued. Half a continent had taken up arms and they meant to rid themselves of European tyrants. The North American continent belonged to those who sweated for it, the colonists. No longer were they French or Spanish or English, they were Americans, and the continent belonged to Americans. Jean duSable, who had brought his own desire for justice and freedom to Eschikagou, must understand that other men also wanted that.

Jean was surprised by Jacques' fiery words. A few years ago when the Spaniards took over Louisiana Jacques had not felt this way, but now that Spain and England were putting the squeeze on Frenchmen, his attitude had changed drastically. Jean was tempted to remind his friend of this but thought better of it.

"I have come to realize the truth of your words, Jean," Clemorgan said. "We should not accept the harsh rules of foreign kings. The continent is expanding. St. Louis grows, and more and more people come to the Mississippi valley. We should be able to operate without interference. The continent has been good to me and now I recognize a duty to make it free —by joining the American colonists."

Jean was glad to learn that Jacques now considered some things more important than money, but doubted that anything could be gained by joining the American cause. He himself was happily settled at Eschikagou, he told Clemorgan, and had received assurances from the British that neither he nor any of the Indians on Des Plaines would be molested so long as the residents remained neutral. He suggested that Jacques remain in Eschikagou where they could renew their old partnership.

"I appreciate the offer," Jacques said, "but I must join the Revolution. I had hoped that you too would join those who seek the same security and peace that you found for yourself."

No, Jean answered, the Revolution by English colonists was none of his concern, nor was it an affair for the Potawatomis. He had struggled hard to bring accomplishment to Eschikagou and he now intended to enjoy with his wife and children the fruits of these efforts. Virginia, far to the east beyond the Appalachian Mountains, lay in another world and meant nothing to Jean duSable.

"But you know you cannot trust the British," Clemorgan said. "Can you say for certain they will not come to Eschikagou?"

"I have had assurances from Colonel de Peyster. If he keeps his word, we at Eschikagou will remain neutral. And I see no reason why he shouldn't keep his word."

The talks now ceased, for both men knew further discussions were useless.

Clemorgan felt disappointed in his Haitian friend, one who

had always insisted on equal treatment for all and been willing to fight for it. But now that he enjoyed snug comfort and influence at Eschikagou the Negro apparently no longer cared about the plight of others. Jacques coldly declined an invitation to remain in Eschikagou for a couple of weeks and the very next day prepared to return to St. Louis to close up his trading post until after the rebellion ended. God willing, the British and Spaniards would soon be gone from the continent. And although Jean tried to soften his friend's bitter disappointment by promising to consider the idea of joining the American colonists Jacques knew he had no such intention.

Catherine stood at Jean's side to wave goodby from the banks of Des Plaines River. When Jacques' canoe slipped around a bend they started home, Catherine strangely silent with a sulky look on her face, occasionally throwing glances at her husband to show her disappointment in his decision.

"I'm sorry, Catherine," Jean said irritably, "but why should we get involved in this foolish squabble between Englishmen?"

Catherine did not answer, but her dark eyes continued to reflect disappointment. She desired peace and security for her family as did any mother but an inbred suspicion of redcoats, nurtured for a lifetime, was stronger. She was willing to see her husband risk death in battle if such a risk would drive the British from the Great Lakes.

"Well?" Jean barked, miffed by Catherine's silence.

"You must do what you believe is right, dearest husband," Catherine answered softly.

The specter of the American Revolution appeared again for Jean duSable only a few weeks after Jacques' embittered departure. Resting leisurely on the veranda of his house, he saw two pirogues pull into one of his Lake Michigan docks. Men, women, and children were in them and what looked to be household goods of a family on the move instead of a trapper's or merchant's baggage. Frowning, Jean walked to the lakeshore as the pirogues docked. One of the white men walked up to the Negro.

"You are Jean Baptiste Pointe duSable?" he asked.

"Yes," Jean answered.

"I am Jean LeLime. I come from Quebec with my family. My companion is Antoine Ouillemette who also comes from Quebec. We owned farms on the St. Lawrence River."

LeLime explained that hostilities between England and her American colonists had brought difficult times to Quebec. Despite the fact that Canadians looked upon the Revolution as a squabble between Englishmen, the British now had become suspicious of all men of French heritage and passed harsh rules limiting travel, disallowing free assembly, and burdening Canadians with heavy taxes to support the war against the colonists. Many Canadians felt trapped. However, LeLime had heard of Des Plaines where a fellow Frenchman ran a trading post and colony, and also that honest men could settle on the rich farmlands and work in peace, without interference from the British. LeLime and Ouillemette had gambled and made the long harsh journey through the Great Lakes. Anything was better than living under the suspicious eyes of the British. Could LeLime and Ouillemette settle here? They would gladly pay for land.

The proposal took Jean duSable by surprise. Whatever else he thought of Eschikagou, he had never looked upon Des Plaines as a place for immigration by Canadian farmers. True, many Frenchmen had settled throughout the Mississippi and Ohio valleys or on the flatlands of Illinois and Indiana, but they had come north from New Orleans or southern Louisiana. Jean had never known any Quebec settlers migrating further west than Lake Ontario or Lake Huron. He had no answer for Jean LeLime. Eschikagou belonged to the Potawatomis. DuSable himself resided here only through the generosity of these Indians.

"Mr. LeLime," Jean said, "it's true that I have a home and trading post here, but no part of Eschikagou is mine to sell or to give away. Land for new farms abounds on Des Plaines but you must obtain land from the Potawatomis, not from me. Their main camp is on the St. Joseph River."

"Please, Mr. duSable," LeLime said, "don't ask us to return to the St. Lawrence River. We gave up everything we owned in Quebec. We've sapped the strength of ourselves and our families to make this voyage to Des Plaines. Surely you can persuade the Indians. We will do anything to settle here. We will harm no one and we will pay for the land as soon as we can."

Jean, sympathetic by nature, could not turn away these Canadians. He talked to Catherine who told him to simply act in good conscience; she had enjoyed a good life here and disliked denying the same opportunity to others. Catherine was a Potawatomi princess and who would question her? So Jean gave LeLime and Ouillemette ten-acre plots of land, pending Potawatomi approval.

Jean duSable grinned as LeLime worked eagerly and excitedly building a cabin for his family. "I'm sure Chief Pokagon will allow you to settle here."

"Mr. duSable," LeLime said, "will the Potawatomis also find room for others? More Canadians will surely follow us to escape the severe laws that have now come to Quebec."

The idea of more Canadians coming to Eschikagou excited Jean. Within a week he left for the St. Joseph to consult with Chief Pokagon and the council chiefs. The Potawatomi leaders already knew of the two Canadian families at Eschikagou, an Indian runner having brought them the news. Jean told Chief Pokagon that Catherine had offered no objections, so he had taken it upon himself to give the refugees plots of land; LeLime and Ouillemette simply desired a free and peaceful life, meaning no harm, and they would pay for the land as soon as they could. However, Jean LeLime had hinted that other immigrants might follow as soon as news got back to the St. Lawrence valley. What course should Jean and the Potawatomis at Eschikagou follow if other men sought asylum on Des Plaines? The country did belong to the Potawatomis. Jean himself had no right to make decisions about its settlement.

"Honored Peacemaker," one of the council subchiefs said,

"what are your thoughts on allowing the Quebec white men to settle at Eschikagou?" Jean looked at Chief Pokagon who merely nodded, indicating he should answer for himself. As duSable hesitated, the subchief spoke again. "Will these white men from Quebec bring to the country the same good as did the honored friend of Pontiac?"

Now Jean answered. "Many Frenchmen have settled on the lands of the Midwest. There is no evidence that they have ever harmed or cheated the Indian. I believe that men like Jean LeLime and Antoine Ouillemette merely desire the same peaceful life for their families as did the Frenchmen from the south. I do not think that honest Canadians will steal the lands of the Potawatomis or rob the Indians of their goods."

"I believe that Jean duSable speaks wisely," Chief Pokagon said. "But I will heed the wishes of the St. Joseph council."

The council at St. Joseph then discussed the problem for two days. Most of them saw no harm in allowing Canadians to settle at Eschikagou. The Potawatomis were, after all, traditional friends of the French and enemies of the British. One subchief pointed out that Frenchmen who lived on his tribal lands had never given him any trouble. Even legends told of the great good that Quebec Frenchmen had brought to the Potawatomis a century ago. Did they not bring tools? And did they not build the chapel of the Black Robes where Potawatomis still prayed to the Christian Great Spirit? After all, there was plenty of land on the Eschikagou plain and the Potawatomis should not deny opportunity to trustworthy Canadians.

"Honored brother of Pontiac," Chief Pokagon said in the council lodge after the decision, "you have taught us to love and respect one another. We could not do anything less for your fellow Frenchmen. We will allow Canadians to settle at Eschikagou. We leave to you the task of apportioning land and collecting payments for these lands."

Over the next year nearly a hundred Canadian families followed Jean LeLime and Antoine Ouillemette to the Midwest, most of them vegetable or dairy farmers, but some trappers and lumbermen. The majority settled on fertile Des Plaines, but some families settled on the lands south of the portage along the Illinois River. However, all of them remained close enough to Des Plaines to take advantage of Jean's blacksmith shop, grist mill, dairy house, trading post and other conveniences.

With the settlement of white Canadians around Eschikagou, Jean duSable's business increased, the white seeking more goods and services than the simple Indian and drawing more travelers across Des Plaines. He was forced to build a wing on his trading post to stock more merchandise, make more frequent trips to Detroit to buy wholesale goods and employ more help. So, besides Choctaw, he hired Jean Le-Lime as a full-time employee. The Canadian left the operation of his farm to his family and during Jean's absences on business trips shared with Choctaw or even Catherine the running of the various enterprises.

On his visits to Detroit Jean often held talks with Colonel Arent Schuyler de Peyster who now divided his time between Fort Michilimackinac and Fort Detroit. He always found the colonel friendly and hospitable and made a special effort to stay on good terms with him because he knew that Colonel de Peyster was aware of the Canadian immigration to the Eschikagou area. On one occasion he asked the officer point blank whether or not these migrations might bring disfavor from the British.

De Peyster had shrugged. "The lands are occupied by the Potawatomis. If they don't mind Canadian farmers settling on these lands, why should we? The crown might be concerned if the Potawatomis harbored traitors who have fled Quebec to avoid just prosecution but as far as we know there is no evidence of this. So, I would not worry about any trouble from the British."

The colonel, in fact, even praised Jean for the growth in farms around the Great Lakes portage. "It's what we need. Permanent settlements bring civilization with them."

Jean told the colonel that no one in the Eschikagou area,

Indian or Canadian, was doing anything anti-British. The Pot-awatomi council of chiefs had agreed to maintain a strict neutrality in Eschikagou and elsewhere during this conflict between Britain and her colonies.

"Fine, fine," de Peyster had said.

With each new visit, Jean came away from the colonel a little more relieved, certain he had won the confidence of the British commander and no longer worried about interference from the British crown.

By the fall of 1777 Jean duSable's enterprises at Eschikagou were humming. Both the trading post and portage service thrived. Indians and Canadians taxed Jean's grist mill, blacksmith shop, smokehouse, and dairy house. LeLime and Choctaw appeared happy and satisfied in his employ and both had proven themselves honest and reliable. The settlers themselves, Canadians and Indians alike, had produced abundant crops during the summer. Many had started dairy and beef herds of their own and some had even built their own dairy houses and smokehouses. Eschikagou exported an overflow of corn, milk, cheeses, and beef to waiting markets in Louisiana and Quebec. Jean duSable could not have been more content, especially since his wife and children were happy, healthy, and contented.

But one morning in October, as Jean watched a Canadian mother and two children meander along an Eschikagou trail, he suddenly realized that an important need was missing in Eschikagou. Dozens of children living on the plains had no school such as the mission schools in Detroit or St. Louis. The Canadians, Catholics as were Jean and many of the Potawatomis, had no church in which to worship. He himself had not attended mass since he left St. Louis several years ago. Surely, the thriving community of Eschikagou deserved a church and school as much as any other growing settlement.

The Negro talked to the Canadians. Would they like a church and mission school here if he could persuade a priest to come? Almost as one, the Quebec Frenchmen said they would support such a mission, both financially and with manual labor, having often discussed among themselves the need for one. They wanted a school for their children, a church for worship, and a priest for their spiritual needs and guidance.

Jean duSable thought about the problem for several days and then wrote a letter to Father Gibault who now worked for Father Lusson in the Catholic mission at Cahokia.

Dear Father,

All goes well in Eschikagou. Your prayers for us have been answered. God has brought us abundance from the soil, peace among the residents, and prosperity for all. Both the Indian and Canadian settlers, who have sought escape from British injustice in Quebec, live here in harmony and security. My wife and children are healthy and happy. I have been repaid a thousand times for the little money I gave to your mission house.

But our wonderful Des Plaines lacks the most important need of all—Christian counsel and education. We have many good Catholic families here, not only Canadians but Potawatomis who still pray in their own way to our Christian God. We need a church and a priest to serve our needs; we need a school to teach our children to read and write. We have a showcase of rich farms, homes, and other material things but no church in which to thank God, and no priest to remind us to be modest and grateful.

You once told me that God planned great things for me if I did not turn bitter. God did direct me and I hope I did not fail Him. You also told me that sometime God puts us here to benefit others rather than ourselves. Could these same words apply to you, dear Father?

As much as you do good works at your mission, Cahokia does not lack a priest, church, and school. We do. Dear Father Gibault, could you find it in your heart to come to Des Plaines and establish a mission school and church? You will find every man, woman and child in this settlement eager to help you. Perhaps you might even finish the task of Father Allouez and Father Charlevoix to complete the Christianization of the Potawatomi Indians.

However, if you feel your work in Cahokia is more im-

92

*portant, I will understand. Already, I owe you more than I
can repay for your comforting counsel and encouragement.
Therefore, I would not think any less of you if you did not
come.*

*Gratefully,
Jean Baptiste Pointe duSable*

Father Gibault read the letter with a mixture of surprise
and eagerness, happy that Jean had not allowed material success to drive God from his mind. As a missionary, the priest
felt duty-bound to go where needed most so, with the approval of Father Lusson, he left immediately for New Orleans
to see his bishop. The Bishop offered no objections, in fact
admired Father Gibault's willingness to leave the comforts of
Cahokia for the hardship of the wilderness and he gave him
his blessing.

Within a month Jean had his reply: Father Pierre Gibault
would come to Des Plaines and do what he could for the settlement. The good father closed the letter with, "Besides, I
must come to Des Plaines if for no other reason than to
Christianize your heathen marriage."

Jean duSable grinned. He took a stroll with Catherine and
his two toddlers. "When the good father arrives," he told his
wife, "we will lack for nothing on the plains of Eschikagou."

"Perhaps it is the will of the Great Spirit, my dearest husband," Catherine answered.

Chapter Ten

By 1778 the Revolutionary War had worsened for England. The defeat at Saratoga, the surprising loss of Trenton, and the naval victory of John Paul Jones had given new confidence to the fledgling American government. Washington's army had chased the British from almost every part of the northern colonies, England still holding the two major cities of New York and Philadelphia only because of its superior navy. Worst of all, the American victories had persuaded France to join the American cause.

Sir Henry Clinton, the commanding general of all British forces in North America, desperately sought a means to slow down the Americans. The British still maintained a stranglehold on the territories west of the Appalachian Mountains, and, because of the continued allegiance of the Miami and Illinois Indians, such strongholds as Fort Niagara, Fort Detroit, Fort Duquesne, and the Lake Huron post of Fort Michilimackinac. So, Clinton turned to the west and Colonel Arent Schuyler de Peyster.

De Peyster responded by pointing out to the Miami and Illinois tribes how unjust was the treaty of a decade ago with the Ottawas and their Potawatomi allies. Weren't the Ottawas their centuries-old enemies? And, by being friends of the French who had now joined the Americans, didn't that make the Americans enemies as well? Help England and she would get back for them the lands around the Great Lakes.

The two tribes had needed little prodding.

Colonel de Peyster encouraged the Illinois and Miami war parties to attack the American frontier settlements in western Pennsylvania, western New York and Virginia to force General George Washington to send troops into the west and relieve the pressure on British troops in New York, Philadelphia, and the southern colonies.

De Peyster's strategy worked too well. Washington called on a burly barrel-chested frontier soldier from Virginia, Colonel George Rogers Clark. The red-bearded Clark took a small force of 200 sharpshooters into the Midwest—rugged dedicated men who proved more than a match for the marauding Indians. The frontiersmen followed Clark anywhere; they willingly attacked Indian bands that outnumbered them three and four to one.

The Miami and Illinois, now facing the deadeye musket barrels of calm frontier soldiers instead of the disorganized defenses of frightened settlers, met with one defeat after another and Indian village after village sued for peace. Clark had even captured the British outposts of Fort Cahokia, Fort Kaskaskia, and Fort Vincennes. Many French settlers, traditionally anti-British, eagerly joined his rugged American band. By late summer of 1778, Clark had scourged the Mississippi and Ohio valleys.

The British panicked, wondering how to cope with this plague from Virginia. Clark in turn wondered where to strike next. Both Colonel Arent Schuyler de Peyster and Colonel George Rogers Clark looked in the same northeasterly direction—Eschikagou!

The strategic portage on the Great Lakes-Mississippi water route was the key to control of the Midwest. If the Brit-

95

ish occupied Eschikagou, they could defend the mid-continent even though they lost the eastern colonies; if it were the Americans, British posts to the east and south would crumple in a giant squeeze. More important, in the harsh Revolutionary War where the wilderness offered very little to marching armies, any military commander could envy the Eschikagou portage as a base. The settlement had grown into a bustling community. Besides the hundred or more French Canadian families who had migrated there from Quebec, a full Potawatomi tribe had now settled at Eschikagou. On the plains cattle, hogs, and other domesticated livestock romped in fat herds. Corn and wheat fields swayed in the breeze, acre after acre. Fruit orchards extended from the Eschikagou River to the Illinois River. Not only homes but also sawmills, poultry houses, a blacksmith shop, dairy barns, and other commercial buildings dotted the settlement. Father Gibault's mission also thrived. Canadian and Indian youngsters daily jammed the mission school, and the pews of his church sagged from the crowds of worshippers who attended Mass every Sunday. Father Gibault was happily carrying out Father Allouez's missionary dream of Christianizing the Potawatomis.

Jean duSable, thankful and grateful for the bounty God had brought to Eschikagou, had shrugged off each piece of news on the American Revolution as none of his business, only concerning himself with the wholesale merchants in Quebec and Detroit who sold him goods. The Haitian was naive enough to think that British and American leaders would ignore this strategic crossroads linking the Atlantic Ocean with the Gulf of Mexico.

The first shock came in late August of 1778. Jean duSable was examining that year's fine corn crop when an Indian farmer tapped him on the shoulder and pointed to the south. When Jean looked up he saw a party of horsemen, perhaps a dozen men, emerging on the flats of Des Plaines. He straightened, rubbed his face, gestured to the Indian to resume his chores, and then hurried out of the cornfield toward the rambling lodging house on the Eschikagou River. By the time he got there, the riders had turned their mounts toward the log building. Jean eyed them with suspicion. They wore no uniforms but, all carried rifles and ammunition belts draped their shoulders. One heavyset man with the thick red beard smiled at Jean.

"My name is Clark," he said. "George Rogers Clark. You must be Jean duSable."

Jean nodded. Then he retreated slightly, bumping into Choctaw who had suddenly come out of the lodging house with two rifles. The Indian handed one gun to Jean and cradled the second in his arms.

Clark smiled again and pointed to the rifle in Jean's hand. "There's no need for that. We've come in peace." But the Negro remained motionless and Clark now looked at the sign above the door: BIEN-VENUE À DES PLAINES. "Ain't that sign supposed to mean hospitality? We could do with a little fresh water and a place to rest a spell."

Jean squeezed his face, angry with himself. No matter who these visitors were or what they wanted, they deserved whatever comforts he could offer. He lowered his rifle and cocked his head at Choctaw who disappeared through the doorway.

Within a few minutes George Rogers Clark and three of his men had seated themselves about the oak table in the parlor of Jean's lodging house. Catherine brought them cool milk and biscuits. The four Virginians wolfed the food while Jean sat rigidly in his chair and studied them, for a moment forgetting they were soldiers. Finally, Clark settled back in his chair and tapped his stomach.

"Ah," he said, "Clemorgan didn't lie about your hospitality."

Jean frowned. Clemorgan! He remembered last year when Jacques told him he would join Virginia in the Revolution, his attempt to convince him that only the Americans could bring freedom and justice to North America, and his disbelief that anyone could view the rebellion as a simple dispute between Englishmen. Now Jean grew wary. Clark had obviously intended to use Jean's friendship with his Haitian friend as leverage.

"What do you know of Clemorgan?"

"Why, haven't you heard?" Clark asked in surprise. "Jacques Clemorgan is an officer in the Virginia militia. He's an intelligent man who knows about British injustice and he'll do his part in helping us rid ourselves of their rule. He said that you knew about British injustice, too, and that maybe you'd be willin' to help us."

Jean simply listened as the red-bearded Clark continued. He told him the British had attacked several Ottawa villages around Lakes Erie and Huron as a warning because of the Ottawas' friendship with the French, and sent Illinois and Miami bands against the Ottawas and Potawatomis. Chief Pokagon was quite upset. The British might persecute the Potawatomis just as they had persecuted Ottawa tribes. Didn't Jean duSable feel any duty to prevent such attacks on his Potawatomi friends? Clark went on to warn that, because France had come to the aid of the Americans, the Canadian farmers here at Eschikagou, the Indians and even Jean himself might be considered traitors to England.

Clark's arguments failed to move Jean duSable. He enjoyed complete freedom at Eschikagou as did all men here. Settlers lived a prosperous life without interference from the British. Why should they fight in a war that was none of their business?

None need fight, Clark explained, merely allow the Americans to build a fort on the Eschikagou River and garrison it with a detachment of American soldiers who could then use Eschikagou as a base of operations against the British in the Midwest. Chief Pokagon had agreed to allow such a fort if the Eschikagou residents had no objections. Surely, Jean could persuade them.

Jean repeated his earlier statement: he wanted no part of the conflict. He was neutral and so were the residents of Eschikagou. A fort here would turn Eschikagou into a battleground again. Residents would fight only if attacked—by Clark, the British, or anyone.

Clark assured Jean that so long as Eschikagou remained neutral he should fear no American attacks. Disappointed, the colonel rose from the table and gestured to his men. When Jean tried to persuade the Americans to accept the hospitality of Eschikagou overnight and start fresh in the morning, Clark scornfully refused.

"I'm sorry, Mr. duSable, but we have important business even if you have not. Most of us must maintain vigilance to keep our freedom. We must be willing to fight for it. But perhaps Eschikagou is the exception to this rule."

The bitter tone of Clark's words still were ringing in Jean's ears as the Americans galloped out of Eschikagou like angry bears who had been stung by bees and could not do anything about it.

The Haitian pursed his lips as he watched them disappear into the distance and when he turned he saw Choctaw and Catherine staring questioningly at him but they said nothing. Jean squeezed his face and turned away, wondering if he had done the right thing, only two hours later to receive a second and more severe shock.

Father Gibault, atop a horse, passed Jean's trading post, a team and wagonload of Indians and Canadians following.

Jean hurried to the road and stopped the priest.

"Where are you going?"

"Ah, Jean," the priest answered, "we must all follow the dictates of our consciences. You, my son, have disavowed this conflict that rages around us. If you believe this is right, then God will judge you fairly. For myself, my conscience tells me that I must help to free mankind on this continent: the Canadians, the Mississippi French, the Indians, and even the English rebels in the colonies. The new American government has said the truth in their declaration, the need to free *all* men. I go to join Colonel Clark as do these men who follow me," he cocked his head at the wagon. "I will offer comfort in the name of God to those who fight this British and Spanish tyranny. May God judge me favorably for abandoning my tasks here to join in a more important task."

"You cannot be serious, Father."

"Even a man of the cloth must do what he can in a just struggle. Good-by, dearest Jean, God willing, we will meet again when this war is over."

Jean duSable watched in astonishment as Father Gibault and the wagonload of men left Des Plaines, then he turned to look at the rich cornfields and the lush orchards. Had his wealth, influence, and good life at Eschikagou left him too smugly satisfied to any longer help those who still sought freedom from want and injustice? The two men he admired most had gone off to join the Americans. He scuffed the ground under his feet and stomped into his trading post.

At Fort Michilimackinac Colonel Arent Schuyler de Peyster grappled with the problem of Clark's victories in the Midwest. His own troops moved about the fort grounds with doubt and uneasiness. Unless the British won a success somewhere—and soon—their forces in the Midwest might collapse from moral hopelessness. Therefore, for de Peyster the importance of Des Plaines was, suddenly, even greater than for George Rogers Clark. De Peyster had never visited the Lake Michigan settlement about which he had learned so much from Jean duSable and the Detroit merchants, also from travelers who had passed through it. Until now, the Fort Michilimackinac commander had paid little military attention to Eschikagou. Despite the entrance of France into the Revolutionary War he had indifferently tolerated Jean duSable, the disgruntled Quebec Canadians and the anti-British Indians who lived there, and even ignored its strategic location on the Great Lakes. But now, as Clark piled one victory upon another, de Peyster looked at it covetously.

Sir Henry Clinton, his commanding general, hastened de Peyster's move against Eschikagou. Clinton too had heard about the fabulous settlement, the great portage in the Midwest, and as news of British losses in the west filtered eastward to his headquarters in New York City Sir Henry sent a letter to Colonel de Peyster seeking more information on Eschikagou and on the black man who enjoyed such great influence in the settlement.

In his reply Colonel de Peyster wrote: *Jean Baptiste Pointe duSable, is a handsome Negro, well educated, and settled in trade at Eschikagou. However, he is much in the French interest.*

Sir Henry Clinton's command then was short and to the point: *On whatever pretext, occupy Eschikagou and build a fort there for a garrison. If necessary, arrest the French Negro.*

Less than two weeks after George Rogers Clark's visit another party of horsemen appeared on Des Plaines. This time the Canadian and Potawatomi farmers stiffened in horror. The burnishing gleam of redcoats was unmistakable. They had learned to fear red-coated soldiers and wavered between running in panic or standing in defiance. Temporary relief washed them when the English troopers trotted straight for Jean duSable's trading post.

The sound of horses drew Jean from his log business house. On the piazza in front of his trading post he calmly awaited the British, Choctaw again behind him with a gun cradled in his arms. The party of soldiers numbered a mere forty so they had obviously come only to talk. A young British lieutenant smiled down at him.

"Good afternoon," he said pleasantly. "I'm Lt. William Bennett of the Fort Michilimackinac garrison. And you must be Jean Baptiste Pointe duSable."

"You've come a long way for nothing," Jean answered coldly. "As I told the Americans, Eschikagou residents are not involved in your war. We remain neutral. Your Colonel de Peyster knows that."

But Lieutenant Bennett had no intention of using persuasion on Jean duSable. The Eschikagou plain was British territory, he said calmly, and he and his party had come to survey a site to build a fort. They would in no way bother the residents so long as the Eschikagouans showed proper allegiance to the British crown.

The stunned duSable protested angrily that Des Plaines belonged to the Potawatomis under the Indian peace treaty of nine years ago with the Ottawas, Miamis and Illinois. It was the Potawatomis who had granted settlement rights.

The British officer dismissed Jean's arguments. All lands east of the Mississippi, including the lands of the Great Lakes area, belonged to the British crown by virtue of her 1763 treaty with the French following the French and Indian War, when France had ceded all her North American territories to England. Why then had the British ignored Eschikagou for the past fifteen years? Jean questioned. Bennett only shrugged. Merely because England had not exercised her right of occupation up to now did not mean that England did not own the territories. And what of the Indian rights to these lands? Jean still questioned. The Ottawas had lost them when they sued for peace following Pontiac's last defeat by Sir William Johnson in 1766. They therefore had no right to cede the lands to anyone. England, in her mercy, had simply allowed the Indians to remain, and even now in the midst of rebellion she had no intention of harming the residents of Eschikagou. The crown simply intended to build a fort here and bring her territories under protective custody because of the rebellious American invasion of the west. The young lieutenant left no room for compromise or discussion. The infuriated duSable insisted, therefore, on an interview with Colonel de Peyster. Bennett could not have been more pleased. His principal mission was to lure the Negro away from the Eschikagou settlement and thus remove the biggest obstacle for the construction of a fort. Jean, too enraged to gauge such motives, had unwittingly made the young lieutenant's mission easy.

The calmer Choctaw, however, had seen these motives clearly. The Potawatomi said nothing and did nothing as Jean duSable hastily packed a bag, bid his family good-by and rode off with the British. Choctaw waited until they all were gone, then called together several Indian braves.

"Take a message at once to Chief Pokagon at St. Joseph and to all the Potawatomi subchiefs. Tell them the British have taken away Jean Baptiste and plan to occupy Eschikagou. Make haste!" he gestured.

Within a half hour the Indian runners had left the Eschikagou plain. Choctaw then exerted enough authority to pack Catherine and her two children off to St. Joseph, saying trouble was coming to Eschikagou and he feared for their safety, and sending two Indian escorts along with them.

Some twenty or thirty miles out of Eschikagou Jean duSable began to suspect the truth when he noticed that several British soldiers clung to him like shadows. He was under guard. He cursed himself for his foolish haste and demanded to be allowed to return to Eschikagou. Bennett refused. He told Jean that his opposition to British interests made it necessary to take him to Fort Michilimackinac.

On the second day out of Eschikagou, however, Lieutenant Bennett noticed a strange change in the Potawatomi villages stretching along the Lake Michigan wilderness route to Fort Michilimackinac. Choctaw's runners had moved swiftly. Indians, glaring at the British troopers with deep hostility, made them squirm uneasily even though the Indians made no moves to interfere with them. Jean had gestured to them to stay away. On the fourth day, after crossing the St. Joseph River, a new fear struck the British soldiers—Indian drums! A steady boom from the depths of the woodlands tingled their spines, including the spine of Lt. William Bennett. The troopers knew perfectly well that duSable's arrest had triggered the drums and that they faced the possibility of an ambush at every turn in the forest. Jean gloated over their anxiety and looked forward to his meeting with Colonel de Peyster.

The troopers sighed in relief when they finally saw the British Union Jack fluttering in the stiff breeze coming off Lake Huron. Fort Michilimackinac with its high palisades, deep outside trenches and six blockhouses stood like a powerful castle on the Mackinaw Straits between Lake Huron and Lake Superior. The grounds for several hundred yards about

103

the fort had been cleared of all trees and brush to expose attackers long before they came within striking range of the sturdy walls. The brass cannon pointing out of the fort's bastions reminded visitors to the fortress that here the British still reigned supreme.

Colonel de Peyster heard Jean's arguments without sympathy. Eschikagou belonged to the crown and England could do whatever she pleased on Des Plaines. He refused to release him.

"You are French, Mr. duSable, and France has now allied herself with the American rebels. Therefore, we must consider you a menace to British interests in the Great Lakes area."

When Jean reminded de Peyster of his many promises during their frequent talks, de Peyster only shrugged. All that had now changed since the American invasion of the Midwest and the entrance of France into the conflict.

However, as the low-keyed drums from the woods beyond the fort suddenly rose to a loud swift tempo, Colonel de Peyster lost his calm composure. He looked sternly at Jean du-Sable who now seemed confident. De Peyster, rattled by that smug look, gestured to several sentries on the ramparts to scan the terrain beyond the fort, and a moment later they responded with quick negative headshakes. There were no signs of Indians beyond the fort.

Jean duSable pointed a warning finger at the colonel. "If you persist on keeping me here, or if you persist in occupying Eschikagou, your soldiers will not travel with safety through any part of the Great Lakes woodlands. I tell you, Colonel, if you incite the Ottawas or Potawatomis to join this George Rogers Clark, your war with the American colonists will be lost."

De Peyster stroked the pointed chin of his narrow face. This Negro trader might well be right. Perhaps the British did have the alliance of the Miamis and Illinois, but they were no match for the powerful Ottawas and their Potawatomi allies. Yet, he had orders to occupy Eschikagou and build a fort there. As the drumbeats intensified de Peyster was plagued with anxiety. He may have pricked a sleeping giant with the arrest of Jean duSable. And if the prick irritated the Upper Great Lakes Indians badly enough, the giant might crunch through the Midwest, squashing British troops in their wake.

De Peyster looked once more at the grinning duSable and the colonel's face reddened with anger.

"Take Mr. duSable to protective quarters," he barked sharply to an aide.

Chapter Eleven

Colonel de Peyster had reason to fear the echo of tom-toms floating through the forests beyond Fort Michilimackinac. The boom of drums had not only carried the news of Jean duSable's arrest and the British intent to occupy Eschikagou, but the drums were guiding Potawatomi and Ottawa subchiefs into St. Joseph. Lieutenant Bennett had marveled at the stamina of runners who could outdistance his mounted party to Fort Michilimackinac, but these runners had moved slowly compared to the fleet couriers who sped for hundreds of miles through the vast Michigan lands of the Potawatomis between Lake Michigan and Lake Huron.

Within two weeks after Jean's arrest, forty Ottawa and Potawatomi leaders had assembled in the large St. Joseph council lodge. The Ottawas had arrived with a thirst for blood and a hunger for vengeance against their ancient enemies, and their harsh posture rubbed off on the more peaceful Potawatomis now that the British had threatened to build a fort at Eschikagou.

The Ottawas had always mistrusted the British, though

their chiefs labored hard to control braves anxious to make war against Britain. Only through Jean duSable had the Ottawas restrained themselves after the murder of the Great Pontiac nine years ago. Since then a new crop of young braves had emerged who saw in the Revolutionary War a great opportunity to renew their long-standing feud. They would drive the British from the Midwest, the Great Lakes, even Quebec itself.

Unfortunately for Britain, the powerful and influential Ottawas had persuaded young Potawatomi braves to join them as, restless from inactivity, they dreamed of the past when the courageous Pontiac sought out and destroyed his enemies everywhere. All these young men had pressured their older tribal leaders. Now the British had arrested the honor-belt brother of Pontiac. This act and the British plan to build a fort on Des Plaines gave young leaders an excuse to attack. Village chiefs could no longer hold a leash on the young, spoiling for a fight. So when Chief Pokagon assembled the St. Joseph conference to discuss a course of action the subchiefs and leaders responded with the same explosive cry:

"Death to the treacherous British!"

The Ottawas had only reluctantly accepted the Potawatomi agreement with Arent de Peyster to keep Eschikagou neutral. They had expressed disappointment in Jean's refusal to cooperate with Colonel George Rogers Clark. But now that the British had broken their word the Potawatomis could no longer remain neutral. The council listened intently to Choctaw, fuming as he told how the British officer had slyly wheedled Jean duSable out of Eschikagou. By the time Choctaw had finished, the council chiefs were boiling with indignation.

One rose to his feet and spoke somberly, "If we do not seek vengeance, we would be as dishonorable as the shameful brave who murdered the great Pontiac. We would be as dishonorable as the evil British who have broken their word to the trusting peacemaker, Jean duSable. The time has come to act!"

Pokagan himself favored a parley with Colonel de Peyster to

warn the Fort Michilimackinac commander of the conse-
quences for this British act. The young chief knew that de
Peyster understood the strength of the Upper Great Lakes
Indians and hoped that the colonel would see the foolishness
of threatening Eschikagou. He believed he could persuade
de Peyster to release Jean and abandon plans for a British fort
on Des Plaines.

But no Jean Baptiste Pointe duSable sat with the council to
support Pokagon's hope for a peaceful solution. Pokagon
alone could never convince the angry assembly of Indian
leaders to seek amends from the British before declaring war,
nor could he in fact risk more criticism from the warlike Ottawa leaders who considered Pokagon soft for having accepted peace nine years ago. So he led them toward a limited war.

"It is the will of the council that we make war on the
British," Pokagon told the tribal leaders, "and I will follow
your wishes. No one is more angered than I over their treachery. As chief of the Potawatomis it is my duty to avenge the
threats to Eschikagou and the arrest of the great peacemaker,
Jean duSable. I ask, however, that you leave this war to me
and to the St. Joseph Potawatomi tribe. It is the Potawatomis
of the St. Joseph who have suffered insult from the British
and it is our responsibility to fight the British."

"We will all fight," one of the Ottawa subchiefs said.

"While I appreciate your eagerness," Pokagon said, "I ask
that the council allow me to avenge this treachery. You may
be sure that the British will feel the wrath and strength of the
Potawatomis. As the St. Joseph chief, I will lead the first war
parties against them. I will defeat them as did the great Pontiac and if they will not come to terms after our first attack I
will call on every Potawatomi and Ottawa to fight. I will ask
every tribe from the banks of the St. Lawrence River to the
shores of Lake Michigan to take up arms against the British."

Some of the subchiefs grumbled. Anxious braves back home
would be disappointed but these leaders could not argue

108

with the St. Joseph chief. Pokagon *did* promise to fight. And the British *had* made their threats against the Potawatomis at Eschikagou. However distasteful, the council accepted Pokagon's suggestion, but they warned him to make no bargains with the British, no compromises. The young chief should remember that thousands of Indians from dozens of villages were ready to fight the British to the death.

While Pokagon prepared his war parties Jean duSable remained a captive at Fort Michilimackinac. Although Colonel de Peyster treated him with courtesy Jean complained daily about the forced confinement. His business suffered from inattention, his family remained without a father, and his friends worried about him. He warned Colonel de Peyster again that the Potawatomis would not tolerate for long the British claims on Eschikagou; and the Potawatomis would have the powerful Ottawas to help them. Didn't the marauding George Rogers Clark cause enough trouble for the British without inciting the Ottawas? Did the colonel think that he and his redcoats could fight the entire Potawatomi and Ottawa nations along with the American colonists?

"I have no alternative," de Peyster always replied.

And, in fact, the colonel had no choice. The orders from Sir Henry Clinton were clear. De Peyster still remembered the exact words: *On whatever pretext, occupy Eschikagou and build a fort there for a garrison. If necessary, arrest the French Negro.*

"Believe me, Colonel," Jean warned de Peyster, "the Indians will strike."

Days passed and still the Indians had not reacted to Jean's arrest. Even the drums had stopped. British patrols continued to move freely through Michigan. Supply trains continued to rumble between Fort Michilimackinac, Fort Detroit, and other British outposts without interference. The British did meet hard stares from the Indians in the Potawatomi villages, but no Indian had attacked a single British redcoat. Had they merely bared their fangs with no intention of starting trouble? After all, hadn't the greatest of Ottawa chiefs, Pontiac, been decisively defeated by British redcoats? Perhaps the memory still lingered in the minds of the Ottawas.

Colonel de Peyster grew more confident each day, Jean du Sable more uncertain. Even the rampaging George Rogers Clark had not attacked any British settlements recently. Perhaps Clark had run out of steam, forcing to a halt his surge through the Midwest. These realities even calmed the jittery nerves of British soldiers.

So de Peyster prepared to build his fort on the Eschikagou plain. For two days the British at Fort Michilimackinac readied a wagontrain, loading it with tools, supplies, food, and other needs. Along with fourteen heavily stacked wagons the expedition included an escort of two companies of soldiers— one hundred men—and three pieces of five-pound cannon. On October 10, 1778, only four weeks after Jean's arrest, the wagontrain left the fort under escort.

"If you move swiftly," de Peyster said to the train's commanding major, "you should make thirty miles a day. You can reach Eschikagou within a fortnight. This will allow you several weeks before cold weather to build a stockade. I understand that ample timber abounds on the plain, and I'm sure you can enlist the aid of local labor in the construction."

Jean duSable watched soberly as the wagontrain expedition left the fort and disappeared into the dense forest trail beyond Fort Michilimackinac. The Indians had foresaken him. His threats to Colonel de Peyster now sounded hollow and Jean felt an angry sense of failure. He had worked hard, done so much, planned so completely to carve a successful settlement out of the Eschikagou wilderness and now, in one stroke, the British had stolen his dream.

Colonel de Peyster, who really admired Jean duSable, tried to comfort the Haitian, expressing sympathy, explaining that he realized what progress had been brought to the Great Lakes area. He assured Jean he felt no personal hostility, his arrest and the British mission to Eschikagou were merely duties that he, as a British colonel, needed to perform. He was obliged to do what he could to end this rebellion by American colonists. And on his honor as an officer in His Majesty's service he promised that as soon as the fort was established on Des Plaines Jean would resume his life and business on the Eschikagou plains without interference. England had no intention of destroying the Eschikagou settlement, or of harming any of its residents or their properties. The crown never interfered with the business of civilians so long as they obeyed the law; in fact, she encouraged her subjects to work and prosper whether they be Englishmen, French, Indian, or whatever.

Actually, de Peyster added, a British garrison at Eschikagou would increase Jean's business. British redcoats were quite loose with their purses. He reminded Jean of the prosperity in Detroit, Fort Niagara, and even Quebec, where British soldiers willingly spent their guineas.

"You will see," the British officer finished, "by Christmas, you and I will joke over this unfortunate need to keep you in temporary custody. We will enjoy a good laugh over tea in your Eschikagou lodging house."

Within a week, however, Colonel Arent Schuyler de Peyster needed sympathy himself. He was settling down to his noonday meal when an array of haggard men and horses emerged from the forest beyond Fort Michilimackinac and straggled across the cleared ground to the fort's main gate. From the parapets sentries gaped in horror. These were British soldiers: limping, heads or legs bandaged, arms in makeshift slings, faces bloodied and bowed; even their horses hobbled. Those inside the fort opened the gates and rushed out to meet the weary battered party of redcoats.

Colonel de Peyster listened in disbelief as the major related his shocking story. The Eschikagou expedition had moved unmolested for three days. Then, without warning, just north of the St. Joseph River, Indians struck the train from ambush. The expedition lost several teamsters and a dozen soldiers, and the attackers burned three of the supply wagons before the major managed to escape the encirclement and continue

111

southward. After the near disaster the major doubled the number of forward scouts on the trail. However, the train had moved only another two miles when a second Indian band struck from ambush more viciously than the first, the skirmish lasting for two hours. Before the major escaped this trap the expedition lost half of the wagons and a dozen more of the escorting troops.

"And then?" de Peyster asked anxiously.

The major shook his head gloomily before he continued. The expedition never even reached the St. Joseph River. After this second attack he decided to retire to Fort Michilimackinac. However, the Indians continued to harass them, by late afternoon launching three more attacks after first silencing the forward scouts. By nightfall the war parties had burned the last of the wagons and killed or wounded another dozen soldiers and teamsters. Only sixty-eight out of a hundred soldiers and fifteen teamsters had survived the series of assaults, the expedition having lost nearly fifty dead and wounded. The attacks had been well planned, accurate, and devastating. Only one breed of Indian could be this successful against two companies of British redcoats. Ottawas.

Ottawas! De Peyster stiffened and his face paled. How foolish to think he had frightened them! He suddenly understood the truth of his own suspicions after arresting Jean duSable and threatening Eschikagou: not only had he awakened but infuriated this sleeping giant.

"What of the wounded? The wounded?" the colonel barked.

Indians had carried off all of them, about forty, no doubt to torment these helpless men with devilish torture before killing them. The rattled Colonel de Peyster, inclined to agree, told the major to take himself and his men to the fort hospital for treatment. Then the colonel looked angrily at Jean, reminding him that Britain never practiced this kind of savagery.

Jean duSable felt a tinge of sorrow. He regretted the loss of so many men, but said the colonel had brought this tragedy on himself. He insisted the Indians only desired fairness. If de Peyster promised to make no further attempts to occupy Eschikagou or other Indian lands, war parties would make no more attacks on British redcoats.

Furious, de Peyster said forty wounded had been carried off so savages could indulge themselves in torture; he would not deal with this kind of savagery.

The next day Indian drums suddenly boomed again from the forests beyond Fort Michilimackinac. The British reacted quickly, moving to battle posts on the fort walls, cannoneers rolling artillery into positions, foot soldiers scrambling to the parapets with aimed muskets and de Peyster himself hurrying to one of the observation posts inside a blockhouse. He allowed Jean duSable to accompany him.

The redcoats stared intently at the forest, waiting for the Indian attack. Despite the fort's strength and its cannon, no redcoat soldier doubted for a moment, after the vicious assaults on the wagon train, that Ottawas had now decided to assault Fort Michilmackinac itself.

Three Indians emerged from the forest, all three on foot, one carrying a white flag of truce.

"Hold fire!" de Peyster cried.

As the Indians came within a dozen yards of the fort Jean duSable stared in amazement. The man carrying the white flag was Chief Pokagon, despite the war paint that covered him from head to waist.

"I seek a council with Colonel de Peyster," Pokagon cried.

Within a few minutes Pokagon was standing before the British colonel. He explained that a council of Ottawa and Potawatomi chiefs had met in St. Joseph. Since the upper Great Lakes Indians had remained neutral during this conflict between Britain and her colonies, the chiefs were disturbed over this British plan to build a fort at Eschikagou, having expected them to stay clear of these lands. The threat to the great portage had angered the tribes. The council chiefs had demanded war. De Peyster must clearly understand the common mistrust between the British and the Ottawas, a mistrust that now gripped the Potawatomis. Had not de Peyster

113

acted foolishly in aggravating the strongest Indian nation on the continent?

Then why hadn't the Ottawas come to parley instead of destroying a British expedition, de Peyster demanded.

The British would not have listened, Pokagon answered. The successful destruction of a large troop of crack British forces would be more convincing than simple talk. Besides, the council had been unwilling to settle for anything less. Only through Pokagon's personal efforts did the Ottawas agree to a limited campaign instead of launching attacks from the St. Lawrence to Lake Michigan. At the moment only the Potawatomi tribe from the St. Joseph had taken to the warpath. Pokagon hoped that one show of force might satisfy the enraged Ottawas as well as convince the British to reconsider. If de Peyster promised to send no more British expeditions southward and westward, and released Jean duSable, the upper Great Lakes tribes would continue their neutrality.

"What of our wounded? What have you done with them?" de Peyster cried.

Chief Pokagon signaled with a hand gesture and a mass of humanity suddenly came out of the forests. Indians, leading horse-drawn *travois* moved across the plain before the fort. The *travois* carried British soldiers, those wounded in the series of skirmishes several days ago.

"We have long ceased to be animals," Pokagon told Colonel de Peyster.

The colonel allowed the Indians to bring the wounded into the fort and return to the forest with their horses and *travois*. Pokagon stayed to continue his talk with the British commander.

He had restrained his war parties and allowed no unnecessary killing. Would the colonel now promise to stay away from the Indians' western lands? If Pokagon took back to St. Joseph Colonel de Peyster's written promise, then peace would return to the Midwest. The British had already strained themselves in the struggle with the colonists. They could ill

114

afford a second struggle like the vicious Pontiac wars of a decade ago.

Jean duSable felt proud and satisfied with Pokagon's suggestions, seeing the Potawatomi's proposal as more than fair. De Peyster, in his heart, must know that the Eschikagou portage belonged to the Potawatomis, that Pokagon had every right to decide who could occupy the plains. The Haitian expected the colonel to accept Pokagon's generous terms.

Colonel Arent Schuyler de Peyster's reply astonished both Jean duSable and Chief Pokagon. Despite the obvious disadvantage in which he found himself, and the specter of an Indian onslaught, he calmly and coldly refused Pokagon's offer. A military code and a firm obedience to order were too ingrained.

Jean duSable was French, de Peyster insisted, and therefore a menace to British interests. The Negro would remain in British custody as long as was necessary. Eschikagou, as did all midwestern lands, belonged to the British crown under treaty terms with the French 1763. Pontiac had seen Britain's determination to affirm this claim during the 1760's when Britain forced him to surrender in 1766. If his descendants refused to accept Britain's claim to all the lands of the Great Lakes, then they too would suffer the fate of Pontiac.

The British *would* build a fort at Eschikagou and neither the Ottawas nor the Potawatomis would stop them. If need be, the British would escort future wagontrains with whole armies of British redcoats and a half-mile train of cannon. Should Pokagon again attack their troops, the British would destroy every Potawatomi village between Fort Michilimackinac and Eschikagou, from the St. Joseph to Lake Huron, and from Lake Erie to Lake Superior. De Peyster would forget this first assault since Pokagon had returned the wounded. However, if war parties interfered again with British activities in the crown territories, no mercy would be shown.

Pokagon listened to de Peyster's blustery words with a mixture of astonishment and determination. The Potawatomi chief told de Peyster he was sorry to have the Midwest again run with blood but the colonel had left Pokagon no choice but to declare war, which he was authorized to do by the mixed council of Ottawa and Potawatomi chiefs. Indian war parties would now join the American, George Rogers Clark, and fight against England. Pokagon would urge every French farmer, trapper, and other non-English resident of the Midwest to join in this fight. Finally, he warned de Peyster that no British soldier could henceforth travel out of Fort Michilimackinac or any other English outpost in safety. In fact, Fort Michilimackinac itself would one day be destroyed.

Thus did Pokagon and de Peyster end their parley. As the Potawatomi chieftain walked slowly back to the forest, Jean duSable turned to the British commander of England's western forces.

"I have never doubted your courage, Colonel, but have you not mistaken foolishness for courage?"

"Perhaps," Colonel de Peyster answered.

When Chief Pokagon brought de Peyster's answer back to the St. Joseph Council he spoke with a heavy heart. The Potawatomi chief had appreciated the decade of peace enabling his people to prosper. However, the subchiefs and leaders greeted the declaration of total war with enthusiasm. Their young had not known the suffering during the Pontiac wars and they ached for a rematch with the British. The tribal leaders could now return to their villages and unleash the eager young warriors.

Within days war parties roved through the Midwest, attacking British settlements around Lake Erie, Lake Huron, the Ohio valley, and even on Lake Ontario. Indians ambushed British patrols so often, so violently and with such success that the movement of troopers became all but impossible. Supply trains ground to a halt even over the previously safe route between Fort Detroit and Fort Duquesne. British outposts in the Midwest were left without aid or supplies and British settlers without protection and many deserted the settlements. Only an occasional flatboat made it to Fort Detroit or Fort Michilimackinac with food, ammunition, or reinforcements.

The assaults intensified when Ottawa war parties and French settlers joined George Rogers Clark and his Virginians. Together, the Americans, French, and Ottawas drove every Tory (pro-British) settler from the farms of the Ohio valley, from the shores of Lake Erie, or from the banks of the Maumee River. The Ottawas even offered Colonel Clark the right to build a fort at Eschikagou (without consulting the Potawatomis). However, the red-bearded Clark no longer saw the necessity for such a fort since the British efforts in the West had all but collapsed.

By the spring of 1779 only Fort Michilimackinac and Fort Detroit remained as effective British outposts in the Great Lakes region. Col. Arent de Peyster, ordered to Fort Detroit to shape up an uneasy garrison, was convinced that England could no longer control the West. He saw no further reason to hold Jean duSable.

"You're released from custody, Mr. duSable," he told him. "Go back to Eschikagou, plant your crops, and care for your business. Please accept my apologies for the forced confinement during these several months."

"It is too late, Colonel," Jean told him. "Your cause is lost; not only here in the West, but perhaps on the continent itself."

"Perhaps so," de Peyster answered softly, aware that Jean was probably speaking the truth.

The release of Jean duSable did nothing to ease the Ottawa thirst for battle. Drunk with victories and lusting for more, their war parties had all but forgotten his confinement at Fort Michilimackinac. Without letup, they continued their rampage against English soldiers and settlements.

When Jean returned to Eschikagou, Choctaw, Jean Le-Lime, and especially Catherine greeted him happily. His children after several days became accustomed again to his presence. But Jean's business had suffered badly during his absence. The raging war in the Midwest had stopped travel over the great inland waterway, and also the free flow of trade between Detroit and Eschikagou, or between St. Louis and Des Plaines portage. Thomas Smith had fled Detroit.

The settlement itself had not changed. Canadian and Indian settlers still worked busily on their farms, though many of the young men had gone off to fight alongside George Rogers Clark and Father Gibault's mission school and church remained closed. The good father still traveled with those who fought the British.

After Jean had rested for a few days and enjoyed the companionship of his wife and children, he told Catherine, "I will see Chief Pokagon and ask that he again talk with Colonel de Peyster. The colonel will now surely see the uselessness of further fighting in the Midwest."

He pleaded with the Potawatomi leader to again seek terms with Colonel de Peyster and stop further bloodshed in the Midwest. The British had suffered a series of defeats but Midwesterners had suffered loss of life and damage to their farms and villages. Jean told Pokagon that the British, in desperation, had transferred Colonel de Peyster to Fort Detroit to rally a losing cause, and that he had all but admitted to him his cause was lost. He would certainly listen to peace terms.

Pokagon sympathized with Jean. However, the Potawatomi leader could no longer restrain the fire of battle raging within the hearts of Ottawa and Potawatomi warriors. The council of chiefs would never listen to Pokagon or Jean as they had ten years ago. The Ottawas had vowed to kill or chase every Englishman in the Midwest. Even now Colonel George Rogers Clark was preparing his biggest expedition in the West— to drive the English from Fort Detroit. Pokagan suggested that he and Jean support this effort since the war itself had come about to protect Jean and his interests in Eschikagou. Perhaps they together could stop the Ottawas who were participating in Clark's expedition from massacring the British garrison and civilians.

In June of 1779 George Rogers Clark and his Indian allies began their assault on Fort Detroit. Jean duSable had joined the expedition, ready to storm the fort with the others, but neither Pokagon nor Clark had any intentions of making a frontal assault against the strong walls or the big cannon. Instead they established a blockade, surrounding the fort, entrenching armed men in a strong ring. Nothing would get in or out of the fort by land. Other armed Indians in pirogues patrolled Lake Erie to stop any supplies of food coming by water. Jean took up a position in one of the pirogues. At night, small bands of Indians harassed the redcoats by wiggling up to the fort walls and sniping at soldiers or lofting firebombs over the walls.

The investment of the British stronghold continued for over two weeks, reducing the British troops to a state of hunger, exhaustion, and nervousness. The British knew that no help would come from the east to break the blockade; by mid-1779 the American colonists were chasing British redcoats from New England to Virginia and from Boston to the Mississippi River. However, the proud and stubborn Arent Schuyler de Peyster refused to surrender. And, although trapped in their own stronghold, faced with starvation, and filled with despair, the British soldiers and civilians took heart from their steadfast colonel who had put himself on less rations and less water than anyone inside the fort. After three weeks of these worsening conditions, de Peyster still held his house in order. The patience paid off.

The restless Ottawas could no longer tolerate the inactivity while awaiting a British surrender. Against the advice of George Rogers Clark and Chief Pokagon, the fanatic Ottawas twice stormed the walls of Fort Detroit with heavy losses. The senseless attacks only encouraged the British to hold out with new determination. The Ottawas now insisted that Clark and his men as well as Pokagon's Potawatomis join in a third assault. When Clark and Pokagon refused, the infuriated Ottawas marched away in disgust, abandoning the siege.

Without them, the bulk of the attacking forces, Clark could not continue the investment of the fort. The British garrison, who had held out so persistently, might now leave the fort and attack Clark's outnumbered men. So he too withdrew from Fort Detroit and marched his men back to Fort Kaskaskia. This was his first and only failure suffered in the Midwestern campaign against the British.

Jean duSable stood at the edge of the woods with Pokagon and watched the British raise their Union Jack to the top of the flagstaff. He detected the narrow frame of Colonel Arent Schuyler de Peyster standing atop one of the fort's parapets.

"He is a stubborn man," Pokagon said. "It is men like him who prolong this vicious war."

"Yes," Jean agreed, "he is a stubborn man."

But Jean saw more than an unyielding redcoat atop the parapet of Fort Detroit. He saw the English character that would keep the British on the North American continent for many years to come, no matter how many armies were thrown against them.

Chapter Twelve

De Peyster's determined stand at Detroit had gone for nothing. Within two years Cornwallis surrendered at Yorktown and brought the Revolutionary War to a close. The formal peace treaty England signed with her former colonies in 1783 gave the colonies the full independence they had won from the mother country and control of all lands east of the Mississippi River and south of Canada.

The Eschikagouans had returned to their peaceful pursuits, Father Gibault to his mission, and the Potawatomi and Ottawa tribes had shed their war paint. Even those settlers who had supported England filtered back to their farms, trading posts, and settlements, and English merchants like Thomas Smith reopened their businesses.

Once again travelers swarmed up and down the inland waterway between Quebec and the Gulf of Mexico, visitors crowded Jean duSable's lodging house and goods jammed his trading post storeroom. The Eschikagou portage was the hub for the movement of people and goods through the interior of the North American continent.

Five years after war's end Eschikagou had grown to be a large settlement. Seven docks now jutted into Lake Michigan, three of them large enough to berth the sailing ships now appearing on the Great Lakes. A dozen smaller docks bulged into Des Plaines River to handle the parade of cargo-laden barges gliding up the Illinois River from St. Louis and New Orleans. Besides Jean duSable's, two other portage companies had sprung up on Des Plaines, an enterprising Potawatomi Indian starting one and the French Canadian Antoine Ouillemette the other. Jean neither complained about the competition nor did he try to hinder it. Eschikagou had become active enough for more than one businessman.

"The portage rivalry reminds all of us that to stay in business we must offer the best possible service at the most reasonable cost. When my partner and I first arrived in St. Louis to begin a fur company, we found many fellow trappers similarly engaged but we did well so long as we gave a fair price for a good pelt."

Jean's two children, when not attending the mission school, helped their parents in the duSable enterprises. Jean, the younger, now fourteen, stocked merchandise in the storeroom or on the trading post's shelves, drove the wagon and ox team that carried travelers and their belongings across the portage, accompanied his father on trapping, hunting or fishing expeditions and occasionally on buying trips, much to his delight.

Suzanne, aged twelve, helped her mother prepare meals, wash dishes, clean and make beds in the lodging house as well as in their own mansion house. When Catherine made visits to her people at St. Joseph she took her daughter with her, the Indians there never failing to admire the beautiful Suzanne. Chief Pokagon would smile with delight when he looked into her sparkling brown eyes, and never could resist giving the young Potawatomi princess a hug.

These postwar years were happy years for the Haitian and his family but Father Gibault was unhappy that a dozen years had passed without his "joining" Jean and Catherine in a Catholic ceremony.

"It is my earnest desire that you Christianize your marriage," Father Gibault often told Jean. "Always you are too busy; always you promise tomorrow or next week. I know of no happier marriage than yours, Jean, but in the eyes of the church you live out of wedlock. You attend Mass, contribute handsomely to the mission church and school and your children have been raised as good Catholics, but you have not fulfilled your duty as a Catholic."

"I will, Father, I will," Jean always replied.

Father Gibault could only sigh and wait.

By 1787 Jean duSable was forty-two years old. But aside from a few gray hairs at the temples he remained robust, strong and active, continuing to spend leisure time either in trapping and hunting or reading eagerly about events in the New World, especially the colonists' moves toward forming a national government.

On a pleasant summer day that year, Jacques Clemorgan paddled a canoe into one of Des Plaines River docks. Jean could not believe his eyes, but the mutual joy in the reunion was more than obvious to the crowd at the riverbank.

Jacques barely recognized the settlement on the Eschikagou River. Cabins and businesses jammed the dirt streets on which both Indians and whites swarmed. From the riverbank behind Jean's house he gaped at the activity on the Lake Michigan docks and in Jean's parlor at the rich new colonial furniture, a finely woven rug, and the glass-paneled French doors which had replaced the rough oak ones.

The two duSable children met Jacques Clemorgan with smiling faces and open arms, being now old enough to understand the affection between him and their parents. They greeted him as they might have greeted an adored uncle who had been away to sea for many years. Clemorgan, grateful for the greeting, also felt gladdened by the family's mutual respect and happiness.

123

"I am overwhelmed, dearest Jean," Clemorgan said.

He spent two full weeks as guest of the duSables, taking frequent hunting and trapping trips with the two Jeans in the dense tall-pine forests north of Eschikagou where game still abounded. He found young Jean courteous, intelligent and eager and he developed a fondness for him.

Besides the outdoor activity the two old friends had long talks over a good pipe in the comfortable parlor chairs. Jacques *had* joined the Virginians in the Revolution and engaged in many skirmishes against the British. He thanked God that he had not been injured or killed, and that the Americans had brought freedom and security to the former British territories. Although he had become a citizen of the commonwealth of Virginia after the fighting he returned to St. Louis where the Spaniards, apparently fearing the new nation east of the Mississippi River now treated him with more courtesy. His trading post and inn at St. Louis were reopened but his long absence had cost him most of his Louisiana customers and he had had to spend the past few years in rebuilding the business. Now the St. Louis enterprises were doing well.

Indirectly, Jacques said, Eschikagou had accounted for much of this success because the convenient portage had encouraged increased trade and travel through St. Louis. That city had grown by leaps and bounds. Jean would not know the place. Perhaps he should visit the river port to see for himself.

"I have bought land from the Illinois at Peoria," Clemorgan said, "and built a cabin there on the beautiful lake. This allows me to get away from the bustle of St. Louis now and then. Peoria is beautiful, Jean. You should buy some land there yourself and get away from Eschikagou occasionally."

"Perhaps I should."

Then Clemorgan suggested that Jean and young Jean take a vacation to Peoria as his guests, and see for themselves how peaceful things were there. Except for a few small Illinois tribal villages only a few white trappers lived there.

Catherine urged acceptance; her husband had been working too hard recently. She would visit St. Joseph for a few weeks, taking Suzanne. Choctaw and Jean LeLime could care for their businesses during the summer, hire temporary summer help if necessary.

So in July of 1787 the two men and the boy paddled down Des Plaines and Illinois Rivers to Peoria, reaching it one week and two hundred miles later. The beauty and solitude were immediately impressive. Tall pines surrounded crystal-clear Lake Peoria which itself teemed with trout and bass. The nearby woods abounded with deer, antelope, and other wild game, martens and beavers popping in and out of the streams in droves. Yes, Peoria reminded Jean of the beautiful Eschikagou on the day seventeen years ago when he first crossed Des Plaines portage.

He and his son spent two weeks at Lake Peoria, rarely venturing into the woods on hunting trips without finding game or paddling out on the lake without returning with fish. Furthermore, the Indians in the Illinois village, friendly and hospitable, offered whatever they needed in the way of oils, blankets, feed, or other goods. When Jean was preparing to leave Peoria Jacques gripped his shoulder.

"Well, what do you think?"

"Jacques," Jean replied, "many years have passed since I enjoyed such a pleasant change. I will buy some lakeshore property myself and build a cabin. Then, I too can occasionally get away for quiet solitude. Why, I might even till a vegetable garden."

"Fine, Jean, fine," Clemorgan said. "The continent's conflicts are over and now each summer we can visit one another and enjoy companionship and talk."

That very summer Jean Baptiste Pointe duSable bought several acres of land on the shores of Lake Peoria, promising to return the following spring and build a fine second home, a place he and his family could use in both summer and winter. Jacques could help in the construction.

"You must come also to see the change in St. Louis,"

Jacques said. "You would even be amazed at the change in Cahokia. It is not just an Indian village that now lies at Chief Pontiac's old place of retirement. Farms and trading posts and cabins stretch out in all directions. The mission church and school are second only to those in New Orleans or perhaps Detroit. You will come, Jean? And bring your family with you?"

"I promise," Jean said.

As Jean paddled northward up the Illinois he scolded himself for his infrequent meetings with Jacques Clemorgan during the past fifteen years. Eschikagou was only four hundred miles from St. Louis, only half that distance from Peoria, and he vowed henceforth to see his friend at least twice a year.

As they moved upriver Jean was surprised to see a pouting look on the face of his son. Hadn't he enjoyed the visit to Peoria? he inquired. Yes, every minute, never recalling such a wonderful time as that spent in the company of "Uncle" Jacques. Then why sulk? Jean persisted.

"Because it is over, Papa," the boy answered, "and now I must go back to school."

Jean duSable laughed and ruffled the boy's hair.

The following spring he built his second home on the shores of Lake Peoria. Jean LeLime and Father Gibault both urged him to take his excited family along. LeLime would care for the businesses and hire extra help. Satisfied with the school progress of the duSable children, Father Gibault gave them some books to study while in Peoria.

There the family used Jacques Clemorgan's cabin while Jean worked on his own, a two-room structure with enough space to afford relative comfort when they stayed here. Young Jean labored as hard as his father, felling timber, clearing ground, tying logs, while Catherine and Suzanne planned the entrances, the location for the fireplace, for the storage shelves and for the well. They would do the housekeeping and they wanted to have their conveniences handy. Meanwhile, Clemorgan had sent beds, tables, and other furnishings up from St. Louis.

126

By the end of June the Peoria home was completed. When Jean proposed the family should now return to Eschikagou the children wailed in protest.

Suzanne said, "Can we not enjoy ourselves for a few weeks?"

"Besides," young Jean added, "school is closed for the summer."

With a grin Jean agreed. Choctaw and Jean LeLime could supervise the dairy house, saw mill, blacksmith shop, and other enterprises at Eschikagou. Jacques Clemorgan invited the family to visit St. Louis but Jean declined, promising a visit there in the near future.

The duSables vacationed at their new Peoria home for about two weeks before returning to Eschikagou where, for the remainder of the summer, Jean occupied himself with his properties. He made repairs on some of the buildings, including new beams on the ceiling of his lodging house and new stones in the chimney of the mansion house; he planted four poplar trees in the large yard fronting the house, built another wagon for his portage service and finally took a trip to Detroit to order more livestock for his farm and more merchandise for his trading post.

In October of 1788 Father Gibault announced to his parishoners that he was going away for a few weeks to Cahokia. Father Lusson had had to retire to a hospital in New Orleans. A new priest had been assigned and the bishop asked that Father Gibault go to Cahokia to help him get started as he had helped Father Lusson to originally establish the mission there. The mission school at Eschikagou would be closed for a month and his flock exempted from attending Mass during this period.

Father Gibault then made a personal call on Jean duSable. "As I said from the pulpit, Jean, I go to Cahokia to help a new pastor. I hope I can be of service."

"I'm sure you will be."

Father Gibault continued, "Why don't you come south for a while? I believe your friend Jacques Clemorgan has several times asked you and your family to visit him in St. Louis. Cahokia is but a few miles away. You might offer some help to this new pastor just as you helped me at Eschikagou."

Jean eyed him suspiciously. "What have you in mind, Father?"

"Jean," Father Gibault said, "Cahokia was the birthplace of this great portage. It was the place from which Des Plaines started for you. Would it not be most appropriate if you were to Christianize your marriage there?"

Jean duSable shook his head with a grin but his children jumped with anticipation. They had been reared as devout Catholics and they wanted their father to be a good Catholic, too. Catherine, who loved her children, desired this Catholic ceremony if it would ease the consciences of Suzanne and young Jean.

Jean himself did not fear the ironbound no-divorce rule that accompanied a Catholic ceremony, never for a moment considering the idea of leaving Catherine. He loved her as much now as he had sixteen years ago, she maintained a clean orderly house, set a fine moral example for the children, and had encouraged Jean in everything he did. Too engrossed in one thing or another he had simply postponed the marriage, but even Jean recognized his obligation to no longer delay. He agreed to visit St. Louis and to marry in the Cahokia Catholic chapel. The children were doubly delighted: not only would their parents come totally into the church, but they would get to visit Uncle Jacques in St. Louis.

The astonished Jacques Clemorgan warmly welcomed the duSables' surprise appearance in St. Louis. Jean explained that the visit had been unexpected, he did not expect Jacques to lodge them in his small home, that he would house his family at one of the St. Louis inns. Clemorgan protested vigorously: the duSables would stay with him even if he had to hire half the men in St. Louis to build accommodations for them.

He attended Mass with the duSables on the day Father Gibault proclaimed the banns and set the wedding for the following week. Jacques insisted on acting as best man.

During this week he left his business duties to clerks and took Jean and his family on a tour of St. Louis. The town on the bluff, more of a city now than a settlement, had spread out for three square miles beyond the river bank. Businesses of all types lined the main street: inns, restaurants, clothing stores, feed shops, even a printing office. People jammed the wooden sidewalks and wagonteams clogged the streets. Jacques dined the duSables in some of the local restaurants and directed Catherine and Suzanne to the shops where they could buy the latest styles from New Orleans. And, since St. Louis had a small theatre, the duSables one evening enjoyed a concert.

Although Jean was proud of his own docks at Eschikagou they could not match the long rows of jutting piers on the banks of the Mississippi River, as busy as the port of New Orleans. So many barges were tied up here that he could not count them. Besides furs, St. Louis now shipped lumber, livestock and other goods southward to New Orleans. The transformation was unbelievable.

Was Jean impressed with the new St. Louis? Jacques asked his old partner. Yes, the settlement had grown fantastically since the day they first come to it with Choctaw, Jean said. But Eschikagou would grow, too.

"You will see, Jacques. Some day Eschikagou will be the most magnificent city on the continent."

"Ah, dearest friend," Jacques replied with a shake of his head, "you persist in dreaming. True, Eschikagou *has* come a long way since you plowed under the pink flowers of the plain. But to expect your portage to become the largest city on the continent . . . you still dream the impossible."

"The dream will come true," Jean duSable insisted.

"Well, no matter," Jacques said. "Enjoy the good things of St. Louis with your family. Forget about Eschikagou for the moment. You are vacationing."

By the end of the week the duSables had nearly worn

themselves out with shopping, eating, and visiting the sights. Then Father Gibault reminded Jean that tomorrow was the day of the wedding.

"You will perform the ceremony," Jean said.

"If that is your wish."

So on October 27, 1788, fifteen years after he married Catherine in a Potawatomi ceremony, Jean Baptiste Pointe duSable married his wife in a Catholic church, only a handful of people witnessing the small quiet ceremony, most of them unacquainted with the duSables, there only out of curiosity.

Jean and Catherine looked at each other with the same tenderness of fifteen years ago. They still loved each other. Young Jean looked on with pride, Jacques beamed with satisfaction because as always he wanted only happiness for his lifelong friend, Father Gibault silently thanked God. Suzanne cried. After the ceremony Father Gibault joined the duSables and Jacques in a quiet dinner at one of the St. Louis inns.

There were two more days in St. Louis before the duSables returned to Eschikagou. Within the next several weeks cold weather would return to Des Plaines and Jean duSable wanted to be there to prepare for it. He stopped only overnight at his cabin at Lake Peoria to make certain that all furniture, windows, and doors were ready for the winter.

Choctaw and Jean LeLime greeted the family's return to Eschikagou with smiles. And, despite the holiday adventures in St. Louis and Cahokia, Jean, Catherine and the two children welcomed the comfort of their own beds again. As Catherine was preparing to retire for the night, Jean noticed she was in deep thought. Was something bothering her?

"I was merely thinking, dearest husband," Catherine answered. "During all these years, this visit to St. Louis was the first time our whole family had gone somewhere together."

"It will not be the last," Jean promised.

Chapter Thirteen

The two Haitians who had arrived penniless in New Orleans, following the advice of Jean duSable's father in 1764, were in 1789 among the most influential and respected men in North America.

Clemorgan far surpassed Jean in business holdings. St. Louis had grown at a tremendous pace during the past ten years and given him greater opportunity to expand. He now owned several warehouses in St. Louis, stacked with everything from furs to livestock, and operated an entire fleet of barges and pirogues, river boats which often passed one another as they glided up and down the Mississippi between St. Louis and New Orleans. Not only did Clemorgan ship tons of raw materials to New Orleans for sale to wholesalers, his barges also carried back tons of goods to be sold to people in St. Louis and the surrounding Missouri and Illinois territory.

The duSables went to Peoria in the summer of 1789 surprised to find Jacques already there with a pretty new bride named Louisa dePew, daughter of a French wholesaler in New Orleans. He had known the girl for two or three years, ever since he began doing business with the dePew wholesale house. Jean's happy family life had apparently encouraged him to marry and start a family of his own, even at age forty-five.

Despite the aristocratic upbringing of Louisa dePew, she showed the highest regard and courtesy for Jean, Catherine, and their children. Louisa had heard so much about the family from Jacques that she felt she already knew them. She got on well with Catherine and Suzanne.

But, while the duSables and Clemorgans innocently enjoyed a pleasant companionship at Peoria the United States Congress was unwittingly brewing trouble for the people living on the western lands between the Ohio valley and Lake Superior, territory which included Jean duSable's beloved Eschikagou and the beautiful Lake Peoria. The settlers of this Great Lakes region had ignored the colonial government's edict of 1787 proclaiming this vast land as the Northwest Territory. Nothing had immediately come of this law because for the two years following the proclamation the Congress was too concerned with establishing a constitution, so midwesterners had not concerned themselves with the edict, either. But now, with the Constitution completed and ratified by most of the states, the government turned to these western lands. On July 13, 1789, it adopted a proposal for administering these territories, Congress passing the Northwest Ordinance, a system for ruling the Territory and eventually bringing it into the United States. Under the plan, the president appointed governors who would have full authority in the lands. Then, as enough Americans settled in each of the various divisional territories, the homesteaders would elect their own governor and officials. When the population reached 60,000 that territory could then be admitted to the Union as a new state.

Besides these provisions, the American Congress would send land surveyors into the territories to mark out six-mile-square tracts as future townships for homesteaders to occupy. When the population of any certain tract reached 1,000 the township could elect its own local government.

Jean duSable was aware of a new government in the East but had paid as little attention to it as did the Indians and Canadians. Appreciating the colonists' help in driving out the British, they had merely looked upon the new citizens of the thirteen states as good neighbors. The Midwesterners had never considered lands of the Great Lakes as part of the United States.

The first impact of this act reached the Great Lakes in the summer of 1789 while Jean duSable and his family paddled happily back to Eschikagou after their summer vacation on Lake Peoria, bringing with them Jacques Clemorgan and his new bride. When the party arrived at Des Plaines River docks in August they noticed at once a strange quiet among the Indian and Canadian residents. At Jean's trading post the faces of Choctaw and Jean LeLime were tight.

"What has happened?" Jean asked anxiously.

"The American government has laid claim to all the lands of the Great Lakes region," Choctaw said, "all the lands from Lake Superior to the Ohio valley."

Then the Indian explained that the American government had named the lands the Northwest Territory and passed a law to allow American settlers on the lands. The law would allow surveyors to come into the territory and mark out township sites for these settlers from the East. When Jean questioned the report, Choctaw said that Americans had already built a settlement called Marietta on the Ohio River, a colony established against the wishes of the Delaware Indians who lived there. The Potawatomis at St. Joseph were shocked by the news and Chief Pokagon had sent runners to Ottawa, Potawatomi, and Chippewa villages to summon a council of chiefs to St. Joseph.

Choctaw then looked angrily at Jacques Clemorgan, "Is this how the Americans thank us for helping them in their war against the British? Did we trade one tyrant for another tyrant? One who would steal our lands from us?"

Jacques could not answer Choctaw. Although the white man had heard something about a Northwest Territory he

133

knew nothing of a plan to occupy Indian lands. Perhaps the Potawatomis had been misinformed, he told Choctaw, for he could not believe that Americans would steal the lands of the Great Lakes without regard to the residents already living here.

Jean duSable was inclined to agree with Clemorgan. He told Choctaw that he would depart immediately for the St. Joseph. He would try to avoid bloodshed by asking the council to seek information before taking any hasty action. Choctaw and Jean LeLime could run Jean's businesses during his absence, along with a young Canadian named Jean Pellitier who had turned out to be a dependable duSable employee, and finally young Jean, who had finished school and now worked for his father fulltime. Jean's affairs would be in capable hands while he visited St. Joseph.

Clemorgan said meanwhile he would hurry to New York. He carried some influence among the Virginia representatives because of his help during the Revolutionary War, and he would ask permission to speak before Congress and explain the injustice of a law that disregarded all the established residents of the Midwest. He would ask the American government to guarantee freedom and security to Indians, Canadians, and other settlers in the Great Lakes area.

Jean duSable and Jacques Clemorgan remained only overnight at Eschikagou, leaving early the next morning for St. Joseph and New York City. The two old friends said little to each other during the sail across Lake Michigan. When they reached the eastern shore, the white man told the black man to ask patience from the Indians until he returned from the American capital in New York City with accurate information. Jean promised to do his utmost, then he hurried northward and Jacques eastward.

On his arrival at St. Joseph, Jean duSable was met by the same quiet gloom as at Eschikagou. The Potawatomi chief neither smiled nor extended a welcome hand.

"They have betrayed us!" Pokagon cried furiously.

"You have heard only rumors," Jean said, hoping to calm

134

him. "Even now, Jacques Clemorgan journeys to New York City to learn more of this so-called Northwest Ordinance. We must not act hastily."

Now the Potawatomi chief pointed sharply at the Haitian Negro. "You know that I accepted peace when first I met you, Jean duSable. You know that I made a treaty with the Illinois and the Miamis because you persuaded me. You know that I made no war with the British because you wanted neutrality at Eschikagou to assure your own progress there. And you know that I turned and fought these same British because they arrested you and they threatened Eschikagou. Ever since I have known you," Pokagon pointed a finger, "I have done things for your benefit. But what has come from listening to you? A threat worse than the British threat, a treachery worse than the treachery of Pontiac's murder. Is this the reward for peace and cooperation? Do not even dare to counsel me again, Jean duSable. This time I will call for immediate war. I will ask every brave between Lake Superior and Quebec, between the St. Lawrence and Ohio rivers, and from the Appalachian to the Rocky mountains to strike out against these new tyrants from the east."

The rumors of American occupation had generated so much hate in the chief's heart that he had to level some of it at him, Jean knew. He could never persuade Pokagon to do anything in the chief's present state of mind, but promised the Potawatomi that he too would take up arms if Americans tried to occupy Indian lands. Jean reminded Pokagon that he also had a high stake in the Midwest, perhaps higher than any single Indian. He asked to speak to the council of chiefs. Pokagon agreed.

Jean stiffened when he saw the somber circle of faces inside of the St. Joseph council lodge. Fire sparked their dark eyes and redness flushed their cheeks. Some of the council leaders had even decked themselves in war paint. They had not assembled here for discussions but to plan an immediate and all-out attack against the new white tyrants.

Leaders and subchiefs, in turn, rose to vent their fury on

the United States, calling for a war greater than the old Pontiac wars, greater than the recent war against the British. They vowed to kill every Easterner who ventured west of the Appalachian Mountains or beyond Detroit. Pokagon joined the tirade and inflamed the passionate call for action.

Jean knew that the Ottawas, Potawatomi, and Chippewas had sacrificed men, women and children as well as homes and farms in the alliance with the Americans in the war against Britain. Still fresh in their minds were the words of George Rogers Clark: *We seek the same freedom and peace from the British as you do. We will bring liberty and security to all men on this continent, regardless of race or creed.* The Indians had believed Clark. They had willingly joined the Virginian. Now, he and his Americans had betrayed them.

"Let there be no delay," one of the subchiefs cried. "The British and Spaniards will gladly sell us guns to fight the eastern intruders."

The council of chiefs praised the suggestion. Then and only then did they agree to hear Jean duSable, eyeing him warily. Several times in the past he had persuaded them to make peace when conditions called for war. Some of the chiefs had already decided to ignore anything the peacemaker said this time. Amid this hostile atmosphere, Jean took a deep nervous breath.

"Council chiefs," he said to them, "I can see fire flaming from your eyes. Perhaps some of you call me coward, using the title of peacemaker as a brand. But I have always been proud of the name because peace has made us prosperous, secure, and free."

"Do you dare to call for peace now?" one asked.

"I tell you," Jean pointed to the subchief, "I did not spend half of a lifetime making a home and business for my family so others could take it away from me. If indeed the Americans intend to occupy the Indian lands of the Great Lakes, then I will be with the first war party who drives them back across the Appalachian Mountains. I will be among the first to kill anyone who tries to take our lands or properties. Only if I am dead will any man come through the doors of my home without permission."

"Then you will fight?"

"If necessary," Jean answered. "But all of you are now blinded by anger. Think carefully, for you have only heard rumors. I ask that you have patience. A dear and trusted friend, Jacques Clemorgan, is even now hurrying to the American capital at New York City to learn what he can of this so-called plan to occupy our territories. I ask that we await his return before we send out war parties against the Americans."

"No!" a leader cried, bounding to his feet. "We will not listen to you again. We must put such fear in their hearts that the Americans will not dare to venture beyond the Appalachians."

Now Jean spoke directly to the leader. Had he seen any Americans? Had any Americans told him his lands would be taken away? Had American soldiers come to his village to drive his people from their homes and farms and hunting grounds? No, Jean answered his own question, we have only heard rumors. Would it be wise to go on the warpath without just cause? Why should the Indian and non-Indian residents of the Midwest arouse the fury of the Americans unless certain that these Easterners meant to take away our lands and properties?

Jean reminded the Indians that George Rogers Clark *did* help to drive the British from the Midwest. He pointed out that the British in Canada had urged the Indians to make war on the Americans, but the Potawatomis and Ottawas, as well as the Canadians, knew of their treachery in trying to pit Ottawas against Illinois by murdering the Great Pontiac. Would the St. Joseph council now allow the British to pit the Great Lakes Indians against the Americans? Surely, the council could wait two weeks until Jacques Clemorgan returned from New York.

The council grumbled as did Chief Pokagon. But, however grudgingly, they knew that Jean duSable, the peacemaker, had once again spoken wisely.

"Perhaps we are fools, Jean duSable," Chief Pokagon told the Negro, "but we will wait for your friend to return from the east. Two weeks!" the chief gestured. "If he is not in St. Joseph by then, we go to war."

"Thank you."

For the next several days he nervously paced about St. Joseph, spending half his time peering into the trail from the south. When someone appeared his dark eyes brightened; his heart sank when it turned out to be someone other than Jacques Clemorgan. To add to Jean's anxiety, Chief Pokagon constantly reminded him that another day had passed and the race grew shorter, that nothing he could say would delay the Indians one day longer than the agreed time.

But on the afternoon of September 16, 1789, Jean's peering eyes were rewarded. Two horsemen had emerged from the forest, one he recognized at once as Jacques Clemorgan and his heart beat faster when he saw the broad grin on his friend's face. The second horseman was an American army officer.

"All is well, Jean," Clemorgan told him. "This is Major William Marshall. He came with me to tell the Indians himself that the United States has no intention of taking anyone's land."

As they and Major Marshall walked into the St. Joseph village, Clemorgan told Jean he had hurried as fast as he could to New York, obtaining fresh mounts at Fort Duquesne and at Philadelphia to ride more swiftly. Through the efforts of George Rogers Clark the Congress had agreed to hear Clemorgan, even though the rumors were false.

The assembled representatives in the United States Congress had no intention of driving Indian or other midwestern settlers from their lands, men like George Rogers Clark, Thomas Jefferson, James Livingston, and others in the Congress having insisted the law be fair. But after hearing Clemorgan, the Congress had authorized Major William Marshall to return with Jacques to reassure the Indians, carrying with him a copy of the Northwest Ordinance. The two men had traveled almost day and night to reach St. Joseph as soon as possible. Within two hours they stood before the Indian council in St. Joseph where Jean duSable, after introducing them, asked Major William Marshall to speak.

The major, somewhat nervous in the midst of these somber-faced Indian chiefs, remained composed. The Americans had not forgotten the help from the Great Lakes Indians in the war against the British, he said, nor had they forgotten how the midwestern peoples had helped George Rogers Clark during the Virginian's expeditions. The Americans had fought vigorously to rid themselves of British rule. Did the Indians think they themselves would now become tyrants? No one understood better than they the need for security against threats to their lands and properties. No! the American Congress desired freedom and security for every man, woman and child on the American continent.

"But what of this Northwest Ordinance?" a subchief asked angrily.

The American officer admitted the Congress of the United States had passed such a law naming the lands of the Great Lakes the Northwest Territories, and asking Americans to settle here—but only on unclaimed lands, purchased lands, or lands won from Great Britain.

Actually, the American officer said, the Congress wrote this law to protect the residents of the Great Lakes area, not to destroy them. The law, while it would open non-Indian land to settlement, also guaranteed that no land belonging to others would be taken away without the consent of the owners.

"What of this injustice against the Delawares at this place called Marietta?" another chief asked.

The chiefs had not heard the truth about Marietta, Major Marshall said. The Delawares had sold a tract of land to the settlers and thereby given the Americans the right to build a settlement there.

Next, he drew a document from his waistcoat and unrolled

it, explaining it was a copy of the original Northwest Ordinance. The chiefs could read it for themselves, or have someone who read English read it to them. He quoted one passage:

> The utmost faith shall always be observed towards the Indians and other landowners; their lands and properties shall never be taken away without their consent; and in their properties, rights, and liberties they shall never be invaded or disturbed unless in just and lawful cause authorized by the Congress; but laws founded in justice and humanity shall from time to time be made for preventing wrongs being done to the Indians; and for preserving peace and friendship with them.

This document had been written two years ago and reaffirmed by the new Congress on August 7, 1789. How wonderful, Major Marshall said proudly, that his country's first law under the Constitution should be a law that protected men's freedoms, properties, and lands. Did this document sound like one that would bring injustice to the Indian? No! The Americans were grateful for the new freedom they themselves had found on this continent, and grateful to the native Indians who helped them win it.

When the major had finished, the council of chiefs sat in astonished silence. None had questions, Major Marshall had answered them all. Chief Pokagon took the document from the American's hand and stared at it awe-stricken, finally clutching the parchment against his chest.

"Post it in your lodge, great Chief," Marshall said to Pokagon. "Post it where every man may read it and feel secure in the knowledge that tyrants have finally left this land. As for you, Jean duSable," Major Marshall turned to the Negro, "we have added another item to the document: *No slavery shall be allowed in the Northwest Territory.* Never in this land will you see fellow blacks in the servitude of others."

Like the council, Jean too was stunned with happiness, unable to answer the American major, either. Then, one of the leaders leaped to his feet.

"A feast!" he cried. "A feast to the Great Spirit who has brought us such joyful news this day." A numbing echo of shouts erupted from the others seated in the circle.

Jean duSable turned to Jacques Clemorgan as tears trickled from his eyes. "Dearest friend, how can I express my joy?"

"Jean," Clemorgan answered, placing an arm around his friend's shoulders, "sometimes it is good for a grown man to cry."

Chapter Fourteen

Enforcing the Northwest Ordinance, however, was not as easy as writing it. Land companies, granted by Congress the right to promote homestead sites, connived with dishonest government agents and forced owners to accept poor terms of sale, even threatening in some cases to drive them off with the help of armed men, claiming the land as public domain, the residents squatters.

For the first several years after the passage of the ordinance these land grabbers operated in the Ohio valley and in lower Illinois and Indiana. Northerners in Potawatomi country went about their business with a false sense of safety and security.

Jean duSable, now in his late forties, had begun to live a more leisurely life, while Choctaw, his longtime friend and employee, returned to the St. Joseph to spend his last years. Jean's son had almost complete charge of the Eschikagou enterprises, assisted by Jean Pellitier whom Suzanne had married in 1792, as well as the faithful Jean LeLime and Antoine Ouillemette.

Jean and Catherine spent more time together, making frequent trips—to St. Joseph, up Lake Michigan to Mackinaw, or down the Mississippi to visit Jacques Clemorgan in St. Louis, and even to New Orleans or Quebec. They also passed many peaceful and delightful days at their quiet retreat in Peoria where Jean enjoyed the close companionship of Jacques Clemorgan and Catherine and Louisa many hours of leisurely chatter.

Despite occasional trials and frustrations, during their twenty-seven years on the continent, both men were prosperous and happy after a near-penniless beginning in 1765. Jean, besides growing wealthy and influential around the Great Lakes, had fulfilled his dream for a free and prosperous Eschikagou, married a woman who truly loved him and raised two loyal and responsible children. Jacques Clemorgan, though childless, had found as much satisfaction, commanding respect from New Orleans to Detroit, from Virginia to the Rockies; no business house, no merchant, and no official—Spanish, French or American—failed to listen when he spoke. Now that the two lifelong friends could renew a faithful and warm relationship, what more could men ask from this life?

It was in 1793 that the land companies invaded the Great Lakes area. Having been so successful in the southern regions of the Midwest, unscrupulous men came to be certain they could seize land anywhere for profitable resale to American homesteaders.

At the end of his usual summer vacation in Peoria when Jean walked into his Eschikagou trading post he found his son and Jean LeLime visibly upset.

"What is wrong?"

"Trouble again, Papa," young Jean said. "American land agents have forced several Canadian families off their lands in the St. Joseph valley, claiming the lands are public domain. They will make a survey. The territory will then be marked off in township sites and opened for settlement to eastern homesteaders."

Later in the day, Jean met two of the men who had been driven from their settlements, a pair of Canadian farmers who with their families had been preparing to harvest late-summer crops when a land agent with a party of ten or fifteen American soldiers came to their farm. The land agent told them they were squatting on government lands, part of the 5th section of the Northwest Territory. The farmers protested. Then the agent threatened arrest if they did not leave within twenty-four hours.

The families had loaded whatever possessions they could on horses and wagons and drove to St. Joseph. Pokagon, when he heard what happened, flew into a rage. He would deal with these land grabbers, he said. To the Canadians he suggested they could still find available land in Eschikagou where Jean duSable would help them to resettle.

After hearing the Canadian farmers' stories, Jean nodded in agreement, assigning them ten-acre plots of land on the north end of the plains, offering them the use of his own Eschikagou facilities to help them rebuild.

"Papa," young Jean said, "what shall we do? These land robbers will not stop at the St. Joseph."

"No," Jean answered. "I will talk with Chief Pokagon."

In the Potawatomi camp on the St. Joseph that October he faced an angry Chief Pokagon.

"Again have we met deceit at the hands of the white man." The Indian Chief held up the copy of the Northwest Ordinance once so proudly posted on his lodge. "Lies! Treacherous lies from fork-tongued thieves! Will my son and other Potawatomi sons forever face these threats from the white man?"

Jean duSable could not answer. The Negro knew that Pokagon's anger was justified. This latest incident with soldier-backed land-grabbers had confirmed the Indians' long suspicion of white men.

"The Americans have proven themselves as unworthy and dishonest as the Spanish and British before them," the infuri-

144

ated Pokagon continued. "I have called a council to St. Joseph—a council of war."

Jean duSable's face tightened but he did not answer.

"Do you hear me, Peacemaker?" Pokagon asked scornfully.

"I will join your council," Jean finally said. "I have often told your council that peaceful talks were the best way to settle differences. But I also told the council that no man would force himself through the doors of my home without killing me first. If indeed we learn that Americans are wrongly driving Indians and Frenchmen from their lands, I too will fight."

Pokagon's face reddened. "If indeed!" he barked. "You still talk of patience and reason? No! We will not wait for them to deliver more lies to us."

Then Pokagon pointed out that the defrauded Canadians were not the only victims. News had trickled into St. Joseph from throughout the Midwest that these land robbers, with the help of American soldiers, had been chasing honest men from their farms everywhere from the Ohio valley northward.

Jean remained in St. Joseph while the booming drums called Indian leaders to the huge Potawatomi village at St. Joseph. Besides Potawatomis and Ottawas, the drums also beckoned Wyandots, Chippewas, Milwaukee and even the Sioux from beyond Lake Superior. For two days the chiefs sat in session inside the council lodge and listened bitterly to the parade of Indians repeating the same lamentable story. Americans had cheated them out of their lands with faithless lies, broken promises, worthless white papers, and in some cases outright force. After the Indians, white French settlers aired the same complaints as their red brothers before the sober council of chiefs.

As he listened Jean duSable studied the faces of the Indian leaders. Disliking the atmosphere within the council lodge he watched the Indians grow more determined with each new speaker, knowing that not even his own Christian God could stop an uprising. He made no effort to speak, but left St. Joseph even before the council reached a decision. He returned

145

to Eschikagou with a heavy heart and a fearful apprehension for the future of the Great Lakes.

Jean was attending to his businesses in Eschikagou when he learned of the St. Joseph decision through Jean LeLime who had made a business trip to Detroit for him.

"Ah, Jean," LeLime said, "tragedy has come to the Great Lakes. Indian bands—Ottawas, Potawatomis, Chippewas and Wyandots—all have begun roving through the land like the heathen savages of the past, burning and looting wherever they find American homesteaders. They have become more barbarous than the dishonest land agents who cheated them, more shameful than the British, and more ruthless than the Spaniards."

As more and more reports of the vicious Indian attacks reached the East, the United States government was forced to respond to the demands of its incensed citizens who did not understand the injustice of crooked land agents. The Congress sent an army into the Midwest under the command of an Indian hater, General Anthony Wayne. "Mad" Anthony and his troops began a counter reign of terror against all Indians, whether peaceful or not, burning villages, carrying off prisoners, and killing innocent women and children.

The brutality and counterbrutality between the Indians and Mad Anthony Wayne's soldiers raged through the winter of 1793–94, including several pitched battles with loss of life on both sides. The bloodshed throughout the Midwest intensified during the spring and summer of 1794 until no resident felt safe from the indiscriminate killing of both sides. Jean duSable did not take his usual vacation to Peoria but visited St. Joseph to plead with Pokagon to stop the bloodshed.

Pokagon himself now had sober thoughts about the raging warfare. He had come to realize that it might in the end bring about the collapse of the Great Lakes Indians.

Father Pierre Gibault, meanwhile, had traveled the dangerous route to Philadelphia, where the United States government had moved its capital. Congressmen listened to him because Father Gibault had helped the Americans during the

Revolutionary War, and sent two American representatives back with him to speak with Pokagon. If Pokagon would call a council and urge the chiefs to make some kind of truce while they worked out the land grabbing problem, the government itself would call a halt to General Wayne's campaign. The government agreed with Father Gibault—if the Americans and Indians spent themselves in a vicious struggle, the greedy British might pick up the pieces and again control the Midwest.

But, despite pleas from duSable, Father Gibault, and the American government representatives, Pokagon could not put the brakes on the furious conflict. The hate was uncontrollable now, he told them, and it would not end until one side or the other surrendered. Pokagon himself was willing for armistice, but the proud and stubborn Wyandot chief Matchekewis now led the most determined of the warriors and would fight to the death.

Matchekewis, with a force of four hundred Milwaukee-Wyandot warriors, continued to ravage the Midwest, attacking General Wayne's patrols, chasing off Americans where he found them. He ambushed American supply wagons, stole horses and supplies, and burned the wagons.

Nor would Mad Anthony Wayne listen to the American representatives who called for peace; he would fight until he saw Matchekewis hanging from the gallows. Finally, on August 20, 1794, General Wayne trapped Matchekewis and over three hundred warriors in encampment at a place called Fallen Timbers and demanded surrender, to which the Wyandot chief responded with a volley from British rifles. By nightfall Matchekewis had lost over half of his warriors, some by surrender, the chief himself barely escaping northward with a handful of survivors during the black hours of the night.

The defeat at Fallen Timbers prompted smaller Indian war parties to accept Pokagon's call for an armistice. General Wayne met with leaders of the Wyandots, Milwaukees, Potawatomis, Ojibwas, Chippewas, and Ottawas, forcing them to concede outright to the United States certain tracts of land. But, on the insistence of the Congress, he promised henceforth to honor the rights of Indians and other midwestern residents to retain other tracts, including the St. Joseph valley.

Among the concessions to Wayne was a six-mile square of land at Eschikagou "to build an American outpost." The land belonged to the Potawatomis and the tribe had every right to cede the six square miles of Des Plaines as part of a peace treaty, but this last agreement threw Jean Baptiste Pointe duSable into an hysterical rage, despite the fact that no Canadian settler had lost any land and that he himself retained all of his properties at Eschikagou. Fanatically proud after a lifetime of accomplishment, he absolutely refused to accept an American presence on Des Plaines, sensing a danger to his influence in Eschikagou if the Americans came.

Jean LeLime, young Jean, even Catherine tried to calm him. They pointed out that Jean's interests were in no way threatened and that peace had returned to the Midwest.

"Nothing will stop the Americans from coming to the Midwest, my son," Father Gibault told Jean. "You came, Canadians came, and others on this continent must also come. Although we may be of different nationalities and creeds, we must learn to live with each other."

However, emotion had replaced reason in the peacemaker. All his life he had convinced others to act cautiously and calmly in crises, but he himself could not. To the shock of his family, Father Gibault, and the Potawatomi Indians, Jean vowed that no American would ever occupy a square foot of the Eschikagou plain so long as he possessed the strength to stop them.

"They have entered my house without my permission, and I must fight them."

So alone, ignoring the pleas of all who knew him, Jean duSable left family, business, and friends. Despite his age—over fifty now—he paddled northward in a blind fury to find Matchekewis and other renegades. He would now plead for war instead of peace, for bloodshed instead of friendship, for vengeance instead of harmony.

148

He made inquiries at several shoreline villages as he paddled north up Lake Michigan. Most of the Indians, fearful of Mad Anthony Wayne, told Jean nothing, but he learned enough and, within two weeks, reached the remote forest camp of the Wyandot chief.

Matchekewis had been rounding up braves to rebuild an army to again fight the Americans. Almost without exception, the two hundred warriors who had gathered in the Matchekewis camp carried British guns and ammunition, among them a Chippewa band under the harsh anti-American chief, Nakowoin.

The still fuming duSable asked Matchekewis if he could join the swelling army of rebels and bring along scores of Canadians who had been chased off their lands. Also, since he enjoyed respect among the Potawatomis, he could enlist Potawatomi braves to fight. Matchekewis and Nakewoin expressed surprise that the peacemaker now sought vengeance against the Americans.

"They have entered my house without my permission and I must fight them," Jean said.

The two chiefs welcomed Jean duSable but declined his suggestion to attack at Eschikagou. A head-to-head fight on Des Plaines with Mad Anthony Wayne would not be wise. They lacked the men and arms to win such a pitched battle. The Indians proposed instead to harass American settlers by burning their farms and taking their goods, a tactic designed to force the Americans to spread soldiers all over the Midwest. Matchekewis believed that the United States had wearied of Indian wars and might have quit altogether except for the unfortunate defeat at Fallen Timbers. Their representatives had come to Chief Pokagon to seek peace and a new harassment would persuade the American government to again sue for peace, when the Indians could obtain better terms.

So in the summer of 1795 warrior bands under Matchekewis, Nakowoin, and the impassioned Jean duSable began a campaign of hit-and-run terror, chasing off American settlers from one end of the Great Lakes to the other, destroying farms, burning homes, stealing wagons, driving off livestock, and pilfering food. This new uprising failed to win support from Pokagon and other Indian chiefs. The Haitian Negro who had so often persuaded them to make peace could not convince them now to make war. The Indian council had made its compact with the Americans, for better or for worse, and felt bound to abide by the treaty so long as the Americans did not violate the terms. The peaceful Indians agreed only not to aid the Americans in their search for the rebellious leaders out of respect for Jean duSable, the cherished honor belt brother of the now legendary Pontiac.

With each new raid on an American settlement came a louder cry from the East to destroy these outlaws. Within two months after the attacks began the American government declared the Indian bands to be renegades. Matchekewis had badly miscalculated. The assaults on the settlements had only brought new determination—and a price on the heads of Matchekewis, Nakowoin and Jean duSable.

At Eschikagou Jean's family grieved in despair. With each passing month of his absence, Catherine smiled less and less, finally falling into a mood of depressed silence, convinced she would never again see her husband alive. Young Jean and Suzanne, as well as Jean Pellitier and Jean LeLime, shared her unhappiness. Their gloom reached a low point when they were told that Jean duSable's only future now lay in death in battle or death by execution.

Chief Pokagon, himself aging, persuaded the Potawatomi princess Catherine to spend more and more time at St. Joseph among her people.

"We understand your sorrow," Pokagon told her, "and we pray with you to the Great Spirit of the 'Black Robes' that Jean remains safe. We owe him much and we grieve with you. He should not be a hunted man."

Father Gibault also tried to soothe Catherine. "You must be strong. Remember that Jean's future now lies in the hands of God. Let us pray that Jean will come to his senses."

Neither Pokagon nor Father Gibault could comfort her. But

hope did come for Catherine, from the only man on the continent who might sway the renegade Jean duSable. In the late fall of 1796, after Jean had been a roving outlaw for more than a year, Jacques Clemorgan called on her at her Eschikagou river mansion.

"Sweet Catherine," the white man said, "no one feels more sorrow for Jean's unfortunate circumstances than I. For the past year I have not slept well, nor eaten well, nor handled my business well. The distress over my dearest friend has even caused me to neglect my patient wife Louisa. But I have good news."

For the first time in months Catherine's eyes brightened.

Jacques then told her he had been to Virginia where, through some friends, he had gained an audience with John Adams who would be the next President of the United States and had pleaded Jean's case. Adams had listened sympathetically. The President-elect was willing to grant a pardon to Jean and the others if they would return to peaceful ways, promising also to restore to rightful landowners all the lands taken from them by dishonest land agents.

"I must see Jean," Jacques said. "Where can I find him?"

"Go to the camp of the Wyandots on Lake Michigan," young Jean said. "Someone there will surely know. If you can win an informant's trust you will find my father."

Clemorgan left Eschikagou at once to canoe up the western coast of Lake Michigan, taking along two Indians to help on the paddles. To his queries along the way Milwaukee and Wyandot villagers shook their heads. No one knew the whereabouts of Jean, Matchekewis or Nakowoin. Or if they did know they refused to give information. When Jacques met the same results at a sixth Wyandot camp he cornered a subchief.

"I am not an American; I am the peacemaker's oldest friend. I must find him and end this hiding for duSable's own sake and for the sake of those with him. If you believe in your Great Spirit you must believe that only good will come from my finding the black white man."

Clemorgan's powerful plea swayed the village subchief. He

gave him the forest location of Matchekewis and also sent along two Wyandot braves.

For three days Jacques trekked over wilderness trails in the dense pine forests and finally, in early December, reached the perimeter of the Wyandot camp where several armed braves surrounded him before he had moved a yard along the path. After assurances from the two braves who accompanied him the sentinels led Jacques Clemorgan into the hidden renegade camp and up to Jean duSable.

This time Jean did not meet Jacques with any bear hug or dances as he had in the past after long separations. He leered at him.

"Your visit is for nothing, Jacques. Save your words. I shall not rest until they kill me or I kill them. My mind cannot be changed, not by you, not by Catherine, not by my children."

Jacques Clemorgan felt a sickness in his heart. This was not his lifelong friend standing before him; not the man with whom he had shared dangers and comforts, joys and disappointments, poverty and success, hopes and disappointment. Bitter lines had erased every facial sign of love and compassion, an icy glare the excited gleam in his eyes; even the lusty ring of Jean's voice had been replaced by a hostile grate. This was a savage standing before him, a wild black man bent on destruction.

"Jean," Jacques said, "if I must leave this camp seeing you as I do now, please grant me one favor."

Jean merely glowered.

"Kill me! Shoot me dead!" Jacques cried. "I would rather be dead than remember you as you now stand before me. During our long lifetime, I accepted your sulky moods and your rantings; I lived with your complaints and with your stubbornness. I understood that all these passions came out of you because you despised the injustice of some men against others. When I think back, it was your compassion for others that endeared you to me. I cannot forget that I owe you my life. But now, to see you practice against others the same terror and hate and savagery you despised . . . !" Jacques shook

152

his head. "No, you are not the same Jean duSable with whom I spent a happy lifetime."

The stinging words pierced the hardened soul of Jean duSable and awakened a tinge of guilt. His eyes softened and he lowered his head.

"Listen to me, Jean," Jacques continued, gripping his black friend's arm. "You cannot stop the future. You cannot stop the desire of other men to share the same freedom and opportunity as you. Remember," he said, "you yourself taught men to love liberty and fortune when you brought these things to the Great Lakes and to your beloved Eschikagou. This outlaw road you have taken will only bring injustice back to the Midwest, only destroy the prosperity men have found through your efforts."

Jean still did not speak but now he was listening.

Jacques Clemorgan then explained that he had seen the American President-elect. John Adams would grant amnesty to Jean and the others if they agreed to return to peaceful pursuits. As a further act of good faith, the new president would ask the American Congress to pass a law which once and for all would protect the security of all Midwesterners. Any man who could prove that he lived on a certain tract of land and built a home there before 1783 could keep the land —up to 400 acres. Did Jean and the others in this renegade band understand? Any man who could prove settlement on a piece of land before 1783 could keep the land—up to four hundred acres.

Jacques took a folded document from his pocket and waved it.

"I remember another such law," Jean said bitterly.

"Jean," Jacques said, "you cannot blame the American government for the wrongs of some of its ungrateful citizens. The United States truly wishes fairness for all men; they are willing to forget the road you have taken for the sake of it. President Adams, when he is sworn into office, will place this law before the Congress and they will pass it." He pointed sternly at Jean. "Unless you give them reason not to pass it."

153

The last statement let sober truth into the mind of Jean duSable. Suddenly he understood that he could not destroy the hopes of others; if the Congress passed this law thousands of Midwesterners could reclaim their homes. The prospect melted the hate built up in him during the past year and reason rose above his desire for revenge, humility replaced vanity.

The Negro asked the others to trust Jacques Clemorgan for the white man would not betray them. At first Matchekewis and Nakowoin balked. However, many of their followers, saddened by the long absence from their families, wanted to return to their homes. When Jacques Clemorgan further explained that Mad Anthony Wayne had been replaced by a new commander, the renegades agreed to lay down their arms.

Jacques Clemorgan acted as go-between for the peace treaty between the renegades and the American authorities. He selected St. Joseph as the meeting place, since Pokagon had offered to do whatever he could to host such a conference. A new governor had been appointed for the Northwest Territory, more understanding than Governor St. Clair, and he attended the conference promising to vigorously enforce the new law to restore lands and settlements to oldtime residents.

Father Pierre Gibault and Jean's family welcomed him home with joy and relief, Catherine especially, who had prayed to her adopted Christian God as well as to her native Great Spirit.

Eschikagou had changed. A small group of American families had settled on the six square miles of plains granted to the United States. They had built more than simple farms: a general merchandise store, a hotel, a tavern, even a stagecoach station. The Americans had done more in one year than Jean's Indians and Canadians had done in a decade.

Never close to the Americans, Jean saw that these Easterners had brought with them initiative, ambition, and farsightedness. He sensed that the beaver-like Americans would change the Eschikagou settlement into the crossroads of the North American continent, not he nor the Indians and Canadians. The Negro suddenly recalled the statement that Jacques Clemorgan had made thirty years ago:

The future of the New World lies in the hands of the Americans.

Chapter Fifteen

When President Adams signed the Homestead Act, he said: "It was never our intention to deprive honest men of their lands when we opened the Northwest Territory to settlement."

Under the terms of the act, thousands of French and Indians attempted to reclaim their farms. However, like the Northwest Ordinance a decade earlier, the new law was more easily passed than carried out. Under the terms of the Treaty of Greenville in 1795 the Indians had ceded most of the lands between the Great Lakes and the Ohio valley to the United States. A wave of homesteaders had rolled into the Midwest and these newly settled American families refused to give up the lands now claimed by original owners. Fortunately, the government agreed to pay these former owners a fair price or grant them new acreage somewhere else. So tension was kept to a minimum. Many of these non-Americans accepted land grants in the upper Mississippi valley or in the lands west of Lake Michigan.

Chief Pokagon expressed disappointment because the Homestead Act could not satisfy everybody. He opened Potawatomi territory to French and Indians who had lost homes to the south of it and allowed them to settle along the St. Joseph valley or in other parts of Potawatomi country between Eschikagou and Lake Huron, but to stop further American immigration to Potawatomi country, including land at Eschikagou, refused to sell any more Potawatomi land. Thus, the Americans on Des Plaines remained confined to the six-square-mile tract won by General Anthony Wayne.

Jean duSable, meanwhile, was again running his Eschikagou enterprises, once more selling merchandise, supplies, and tools to the Indians and French on Des Plaines, on the St. Joseph, or along the Illinois River. But the Americans on Des Plaines showed little interest in Jean's goods or services, preferring to buy from the East even though delivery took longer and the merchandise cost more. The fact that Jean had been a recent renegade preying on American homesteaders may have caused him to be disliked. He just tried to ignore his American neighbors.

However, Americans were popping up everywhere. In Peoria, Jean found more and more of them settling. The rich Illinois soil had drawn eastern farmers willing to pay top prices to Indian and French settlers for their lands. In 1798, after his usual summer trip to Peoria, Jean returned to Eschikagou to find the latest American influence—an intrusion threatening his very livelihood.

"Papa," young Jean told his father, "our business has fallen badly in the St. Joseph valley."

"What?"

"The Indians and Canadians now buy from a new merchant who has opened a large trading post on the St. Joseph River. He is called John Kinzie, an American who comes from the colony of Virginia. This man not only commands the business of midwestern Americans, but he now sells to our longtime Potawatomi and Candian customers."

Jean duSable frowned, not necessarily in fear of competition; he had met business rivalries all his life and expected American merchants to come westward on the heels of American settlers. However, he had not expected his own French and Indians to deal with them. He told his son he would go immediately to the St. Joseph for talks with Chief Pokagon. Young Jean, however, pointed out that Americans had come westward to stay, would come in larger numbers, and that his father must now compete with American merchants for American trade. They could start right here at Eschikagou by cultivating the American colony on Des Plaines; after all, they *could* sell cheaper than John Kinzie who was based on the St. Joseph, and the American habit of thrift would overcome their disapproval of his recent anti-American adventure.

Jean duSable's stubborn pride made him balk. He would not beg Americans for their business. The Haitian, growing old and settled in his ways, who could not easily accept the swift changes coming to the Midwest, insisted on dealing only with French and Indians. His people. However, he met stunning disappointment when he visited Chief Pokagon on the St. Joseph. The elderly Potawatomi leader shared none of Jean's settled ideas. The Potawatomis had sold a tract of land on the St. Joseph to John Kinzie so the man could open a trading post and, subsequently, Kinzie had brought in horses, tools, utensils, and other goods for sale in the St. Joseph valley, selling these goods at very reasonable prices. The residents of the valley were quite satisfied.

"Perhaps it is well that you need no longer worry about those of us on the St. Joseph," Pokagon told Jean. "You are busy enough with your large trade at Eschikagou and along the Illinois and Mississippi rivers."

"I feel upset at the thought of losing longtime friends."

"Jean," Pokagon said, placing hand on the Negro's shoulder, "you have not lost a single friend. Mr. Kinzie is merely a supplier of goods. Only once did he step inside my lodge and then only to explain his purpose here. He sells to us because he can sell cheaper than you, because his goods do not come as far west as yours. Besides, with the great number of people coming into the Great Lakes area, the country needs more trading posts to serve these people."

"You mean the Americans," Jean said.

Pokagon nodded.

"But you promised to sell no more land to the Americans."

Pokagon sighed. "We have spent many hours in the council lodge discussing the Americans, but there is nothing we can do to stop their invasion of the St. Joseph valley. Neither I nor the subchiefs can stop the legitimate sale of property. Land companies offer handsome prices for the land to our Indians and these Indians willingly sell."

Pokagon, shaking his head, admitted that the St. Joseph valley looked more like an American settlement than like the seat of the Potawatomi nation, but the aging chief had simply accepted the American presence and learned to live with it.

Jean pointed out that if Potawatomis continued to sell land they would find themselves with no place to go. Didn't the Potawatomis think about that? Pokagon nodded: he and the council chiefs had many times warned their people of such a possibility but the Indians did not listen. With the money for the land the Indians bought horses, travois, guns, and blankets—more than they ever had before—then they moved to the virgin wilderness beyond Lake Michigan to start over in greater comfort.

Jean left Pokagon to call on John Kinzie, being curious about this merchant and his St. Joseph trading post. The white man greeted the black man with a warm and excited expression, vigorously shaking his hand. For several years, Kinzie said, he had been looking forward to meeting the legendary Pointe duSable, having heard in far off Virginia of the French Negro who had built a successful settlement on the Eschikagou plains, bringing civilization to the Midwest. John Kinzie praised Jean for his fine work that had enabled the non-Indian to settle and grow in the Midwest.

"I have done well myself since opening a trading post on the St. Joseph," Kinzie said. "The Indians are friendly and helpful. I never lack for customers and I could not be more satisfied. And I, too, buy my wholesale goods from James May and Thomas Smith at Detroit because if the famed Jean duSable buys from these wholesalers then these wholesalers must be reliable."

Kinzie then praised Eschikagou. Des Plaines was the most important place in the Midwest, the white man said, the anchor point for the vast inland waterway of the interior continent. Eschikagou would undoubtedly become the crossroads of America and duSable could take pride in the work he had done there. Kinzie admitted that he himself would like to open a trading post at Eschikagou but—the white man sighed in disappointment—the Potawatomis would sell no more land there to Americans.

Despite Kinzie's praise Jean left the St. Joseph valley with a feeling of failure, his talks with Pokagon and the Virginia trader having convinced him that residents in the St. Joseph area neither wanted nor needed him. He must now concentrate on Eschikagou and the regions south of Des Plaines. He would follow his son's suggestion to seek business among the Americans. He had amassed enough wealth to care for the needs of himself and Catherine for the remainder of his life, but his son was still young and needed to work and earn money. So Jean could not allow the duSable enterprises to fail.

Back at Eschikagou, young Jean welcomed his father's change of heart. Americans were continuing to swarm into the Midwest while French and Indians moved northward and westward. Furthermore, the Americans sought more comforts in their lives and therefore bought more services and goods than did the non-Americans.

"Do whatever pleases you," Jean told his son. "As for myself, I have decided to live permanently in Peoria. Your mother has agreed that I retire and that we leave the business in your hands."

For the next couple of years, however, Jean and Catherine continued to live at Eschikagou as well as at Peoria. He took no active part in his enterprises. His son and son-in-law, Jean Pellitier, quite successfully ran the trading post, grist mill, horse barn, lodging house, portage service, and other busi-

160

nesses. Americans on Des Plaines were buying quite regularly from the duSables.

Then, in the spring of 1800, business suddenly began to fall off. Competition had come from the east. John Kinzie was shipping goods here to Eschikagou and the Americans gradually switched their trade to the glib-tongued trader from the St. Joseph. Worse, as more and more Potawatomi and French settlers on the plains sold out to Americans, the duSable profits became even smaller.

"Papa," young Jean told his father, "we can no longer do well here on Des Plaines. We must build a trading post elsewhere. Since our best trade lies among the settlers along the Illinois River, perhaps we should sell out our properties and move the business to Peoria."

Jean was shocked by his son's proposal. "Leave Eschikagou! You were born and raised here as was your sister. I changed these plains from an Indian battleground to a prosperous community, from a wilderness to a thriving settlement. I made Des Plaines the prize of the Midwest. Would you ask that the duSable enterprises leave the land of its birth?" he asked irritably. "Would you ask that we abandon that which took thirty years to build? I spent the first half of my lifetime finding a place where I and others could live in peace and prosperity. I spent the other half of my life in fulfilling this dream at Eschikagou. Jean, my son, I cannot give up this lifetime of effort."

"Papa," the young man said, "you know that great changes have come to the Midwest during your lifetime, changes that no one can stop. You must accept a painful truth. Americans like John Kinzie have become the new Jean duSables of the Great Lakes. Kinzie has won the Potawatomis of the St. Joseph and he commands the trade of Americans who come daily from the East."

"But I spent a lifetime, a lifetime," Jean wailed, almost sobbing.

"Papa, you have brought peace, progress, and success to these vast lands, especially to Eschikagou. Suzanne and I are

161

thankful that you were our father. Yet, as Uncle Jacques Clemorgan said, you cannot stop others from enjoying the fruits of your labors. Perhaps you would have preferred that our people, Frenchmen and Potawatomis, benefit from your struggle. But it will be the Americans who do."

Jean duSable shook his head and looked at his wrinkled calloused hands. "I did all this and now I must leave it to strangers. It is unfair, Jean; unfair." He looked at his beloved Des Plaines before he spoke again. "Anyway, who would buy our properties? Our house that your mother loves so dearly? Our business that I built with my own hands?"

Young Jean hesitated. Then he said that Jean LeLime, his father's longtime employee, had offered to buy all of Jean's Eschikagou holdings. He would pay six thousand livres for the properties, a fair price. The Negro looked suspiciously at his son. Where would Jean LeLime get six thousand livres? While he had always paid his employee a good wage, Jean could not believe that LeLime had amassed this much in savings and was certain that during his long years of reliable service LeLime had never stolen money or goods from the business.

Jean LeLime himself told his employer that he had saved some money and that certain businessmen in the East had agreed to lend him the balance to buy the duSable enterprises in Eschikagou. If indeed Jean and his family intended to move permanently to Peoria, was not LeLime, a long and faithful employee, more entitled to purchase their properties on Des Plaines than someone else? Jean could not argue with LeLime's reasoning, but he questioned his motives; the duSables' business was showing poor profits.

LeLime pointed out, however, that he had not protested the American presence here, nor aroused their anger by joining Matchekewis' renegade band; he had actually befriended many of the American settlers in the area, accepted their way of life, and could, therefore, draw business from them.

Young Jean and Jean Pellitier urged the elder duSable to accept LeLime's offer. No matter how badly he felt, the Negro must sell; Eschikagou no longer belonged to Jean Baptiste

162

Pointe duSable. He would be much better off in Peoria where he could still be among his own kind.

"I will think about it," Jean said.

Father Gibault had also become disillusioned with Des Plaines. With Protestant ministers coming into Eschikagou to serve the increasing numbers of Americans who replaced French and Canadians, the Catholic mission no longer received the support it needed to survive. Father Gibault would return to Cahokia. He urged Jean to move to Peoria, for Cahokia was not far from there and he and Jean could see each other more often.

So, in May of 1800, at the regional surrogate office in Detroit, Jean Baptiste Pointe duSable deeded all his Eschikagou properties, including the smallest tool and all livestock, to Jean LeLime for six thousand livres. By a strange coincidence John Kinzie had appeared in Detroit on the day of the sale and offered to witness the transfer of the properties.

Jean returned to Eschikagou, loaded his personal possessions and his family on a pirogue, and floated southward to Peoria. Tears came into his eyes as he watched beautiful Des Plaines fade away, fearing that he would never again see his beloved Eschikagou.

Six thousand livres proved more than enough to build and stock a new trading post at Peoria. Jean himself took no active part, but his son and son-in-law soon built a thriving business among settlers on the Illinois River, including Americans. Young Jean and Jean Pellitier found a good supplier in Jacques Clemorgan who sold them wholesale goods at low prices so the young men could prosper. He understood Jean's own deep disappointment so did what he could to help his son and son-in-law. However, the white man also reminded his black friend that he had amassed enough wealth to live in comfort for his remaining days. He should be grateful for that.

"All of us would like to keep things as they were," Jacques told Jean, "but this can never be. Take comfort in the fact that you and I and others like us planted the seeds for this growth on the mid-continent. Surely they will remember us for that."

"Perhaps."

To raise Jean's spirits, Jacques also pointed out that he still had his family with him: a devoted wife who loved him dearly, and a young granddaughter, Eulalie, who adored her grandfather. All things considered, life had treated Jean duSable quite well.

Then, in 1803, three events rocked the North American continent.

First, the Louisiana Purchase: a near-bankrupt Napoleon Bonaparte sold the vast Louisiana territory to the United States for fifteen million dollars. The size of America had suddenly doubled. Thousands of Frenchmen and Spaniards found themselves under United States citizenship. But worse, President Thomas Jefferson decided to send Captain Meriwether Lewis and Captain William Clark on an expedition to survey the entire territory all the way to the Pacific Ocean, a prelude to opening the vast lands to American homesteaders.

The second event: The United States built Fort Dearborn at Eschikagou. The outpost would draw a flood of Americans to Eschikagou and the surrounding area. Not only the old French settlers but Indians too would be squeezed out of the Great Lakes region. Within a decade the Americans would completely control and dominate the mid-continent.

The third event, ignored by American history, probably shook the aging and despairing Jean duSable more than the other two. John Kinzie took over the former duSable properties in Eschikagou. DuSable had long suspected that LeLime actually represented someone else when he purchased the properties; he now felt certain that John Kinzie was the silent purchaser who, with the coming of Fort Dearborn to Des Plaines, had apparently decided to operate the enterprises himself.

In 1805, the Haitian made one last visit to Eschikagou. He did not even recognize the place. The first obvious change, Fort Dearborn, sat on the Eschikagou River like a strange new hillside suddenly popped out of the flat plains. Soldiers swarmed about it, wagonloads of goods and troops constantly rattled in and out of the gates. The soldiers wore unfamiliar blue uniforms instead of the British red that Jean remembered so clearly, and the flag fluttering in the Lake Michigan breeze was the odd one with stars and stripes that Jean had seen only once during the Revolutionary War.

Americans inhabited every part of the plains, the last Potawatomi having apparently sold out. The few French Canadians who still remained had adopted the ways and language of the Americans. Construction of new cabins, roads, and business places went on at a dizzy pace. And noticeably, these busy American newcomers called on John Kinzie for supplies, goods, services, and other needs. He had become the hub for this new active expansion of Des Plaines, with a dozen employees working for him in the various enterprises formerly belonging to Jean duSable.

Besides selling to these new builders at Eschikagou, Kinzie also sold goods and services to the streams of people moving westward to the Illinois and upper Mississippi rivers. Throngs of transients used John Kinzie's docks on Des Plaines River or on the shore of Lake Michigan, moved their oxen and wagons across Kinzie's roads, bought at Kinzie's trading post, repaired wagons at the Kinzie blacksmith shop and, those who could afford it, rested at the Kinzie lodging house.

John Kinzie, despite a busy schedule, welcomed Jean and Catherine when they called on him, even offering them free lodgings for the night.

"We owe you that because you did so much for Chicago."

"Chicago?" Jean questioned.

Kinzie smiled. "Americans have a strange habit of shortening names to suit their dialects."

After a night's rest Jean and Catherine continued on to the St. Joseph valley to visit the Potawatomis. But the old Indian village now lay hidden. American settlers, traders and soldiers were everywhere. Easterners now reigned in the St. Joseph valley just as they reigned on the old Eschikagou plain, now called Chicago.

How odd the St. Joseph looked. When Jean duSable had

165

first come here more than thirty years ago only the sprawling village of St. Joseph, with its lodges and teepees, marred the vast wilderness. Now homesteads replaced virgin forests, cultivated farms the wild grasses, wagon roads the beaten Indian trails. The neighs of horses echoed over the valley instead of the howls of wolves. Wagons rumbled along the banks of the St. Joseph River instead of *travois*. The elderly Pokagon had retired to a quiet inactivity. His son now ruled at St. Joseph, attempting to hold together a tribe in a land that no longer belonged to the Indian. Pokagon smiled when he saw Jean and Catherine, but the changes in the St. Joseph valley had saddened the aging chief who saw a bleak future for the Potawatomis.

"Ah, Jean, the Americans will sooner or later drive the last Indian from the St. Joseph just as they have driven him from Eschikagou. I hope I do not live to see that shameful day."

Jean and Catherine left the St. Joseph valley feeling they had been to a strange land that left men like Jean duSable and Chief Pokagon in the past.

Back at Peoria Jean, like Pokagon, resigned himself to a life of peace and quiet. His influence in the Midwest had come to an end and the Negro finally accepted this truth. He took comfort in the fact that he still had his faithful wife and his cherished companion, Jacques Clemorgan. Furthermore, he could enjoy the companionship of his two grandchildren, especially Suzanne's daughter Eulalie, the bright-eyed youngster who somehow compensated for the loss of his beloved Eschikagou.

He lived in Peoria for ten years, during which time Des Plaines gradually forgot the name Jean duSable. John Kinzie was the merchant of Chicago. As increasing numbers of Americans came to the Northwest Territory, his businesses boomed and his name rose above all others.

The name of Jean duSable also passed away in the St. Joseph valley. A new generation of Potawatomis had sprung up, a generation accustomed to American faces, American homesteads, and American businesses throughout the valley. For Pokagon's son and other young Indians around the St. Joseph, men like John Kinzie represented the Midwest. This new breed of Potawatomis, however, hated the American invaders who had squeezed them into a corner and they made a final futile effort to regain their lands by siding with the British during the War of 1812.

A new leader, a Shawnee chief named Tecumseh, led this newest challenge against the United States. He and the Potawatomis raided American settlements and outposts, burned Fort Dearborn and the Eschikagou settlement, massacring many Americans. But, like others before them, this new generation of Indians could not stop the American occupation of the Midwest. Tecumseh lost a key battle at Tippecanoe and his life in a second battle in 1813 when the last feeble Indian grip on the Great Lakes came to an end. The younger Pokagon returned to his shrunken Potawatomi lands in failure and disappointment.

During these same years in the early 1800's Jean duSable lost his faithful wife Catherine, his dear friend Jacques Clemorgan, and his son. Finally, he received word that Father Pierre Gibault had died at Cahokia. Suzanne and his son-in-law, Jean Pellitier, moved back to Canada. Jean was left with his young granddaughter, Eulalie Pellitier, who married Michael deRoi, and he moved with them to St. Charles, Missouri, where Jean bought a house and a farm which he deeded to Eulalie and Michael on condition that she care for him and promise to bury him with Catholic rites in a Catholic cemetery.

"You will honor this wish?"

"On my honor as good Catholic," Eulalie replied.

For the next few years Jean duSable lived quietly on his St. Charles farm, tending a small flower garden to keep active and spending considerable time in a rocking chair on his sunny porch daydreaming. On August 29, 1818, Jean Baptiste Pointe duSable at age seventy-three died quietly in his sleep. True to her word, Eulalie deRoi had a funeral Mass held for her grandfather and buried him in the Catholic cemetery at St. Charles, Missouri.

Fortunately, Jean duSable did not live to see the final insult to the Potawatomis. In the 1830's the Potawatomis gave up to the United States their last piece of territory in the Midwest and began a painful exodus to Kansas where the United States government had given the last of Catherine du-Sable's tribe a large reservation.

The Americanization of the Great Lakes had been completed, the sprawling community of Chicago, now totally American, become a recognized geographic town in the United States and, mistakenly, John Kinzie its founder.

But somehow, put there by someone unknown, a plaque found its way onto the side of an old soap factory:

On this site, in 1772, Jean Baptiste Pointe duSable, a Negro from Santo Domingo, built the first cabin at Chicago.

And it was that plaque which led early 20th century historians on a trial of inquiry. Perhaps Historian Milo Milton Quaife best summed up the importance of Jean Baptiste Pointe duSable when he wrote:

> *The sober historical record, pieced from many divergent sources, discloses him as a man in whom the modern city may take legitimate pride. From the humblest conceivable beginnings Pointe duSable achieved, unaided, a position of commercial importance and assured respectability. He inspired friendships which were not shaken by fortune's frowns, and he commanded the confidence of men in responsible governmental and commercial stations. He was a true pioneer of civilization, leader of an unending procession of Chicago's swarming millions. Even in his mixed blood, he truly represented the future city, for where else on earth is a greater conglomeration of races and breeds assembled together than in Chicago?*

Bibliography

Chicago Historical Society Library Archives
  Howard, Hugh, "Journal of Hugh Howard" (Manuscript orig-
    inally owned by Clarence M. Burton of Detroit).
Fergus Historical Series, Fergus Printing Co., Chicago, Ill.
  Arnold, Isaac, "Narratives of William Huckley and Gordon
    Hubbard," 1877.
  Arnold, Isaac, "Sketch of Billy Caldwell," 1877.
  Arnold, Isaac, "Sketch of John H. Kinzie," 1877.
  Arnold, Isaac, "Winnebago and Shabonee Scares," 1877.
  Balestier, Joseph, "A Relic of 1840—Directory of Chicago in
    1839," 1840.
  Brown, William H., "Biographic Sketch of Early Chicago Set-
    tlers, Part I," 1864.
  Brown, William H., "Biographic Sketch of Early Chicago Set-
    tlers, Part II," 1876.
  Caton, John Dean, "Early Movement in Illinois for Legalization
    of Slavery," 1863.
  Fergus, Robert, "Last of the Illinois," 1876.
  Fergus, Robert, "Sketch of the Potawatomis," 1876.

Hager, Albert, "Early Chicago," 1876.

Martineau, Harriet, "Strange Early Data (Chicago)," 1840.

Wentworth, John, "Early Chicago Supplement," 1876.

Field Museum of Natural History, Chicago, 1926.

Stone, J. M., "Fall of the Illinois" and "Fall of the Potawatomi".

Strong, William Duncan, "Indian Tribes of the Chicago Region".

Illinois Historical Society

McCollough, J., "Old Peoria," vols. XXI and XXII.

McCollough, J., "Personal Memoirs," pp. 447, Draper Collection.

Indiana Historical Society

Petit, Benjamin Marie, "Trail of Death (Potawatomi)," letter manuscript.

Michigan Pioneer Collection

Bennett, William, "Inventory of Goods Taken from duSable," vol. X, no. 366.

Wisconsin Historical Collection

Bennett, William, "Report on Arrest of duSable, August, 1779," vol. XVII, no. 309.

De Peyster, Arent Schuyler, "De Peyster Journals to July 4, 1779," manuscript, vol. XVIII, no. 383.

Grignon, Augustin, "Recollections of Augustin Grignon," vol. III, pp. 292.

Matson, N., "French and Indians of Illinois (including interview with duSable's grandson)," pp. 187–91.

McCollough, J., "Early Days of Peoria and Chicago," pp. 91–92.

Atkinson, Eleanor, Development of Chicago, 1534 to 1910, Caxton Club, Chicago, 1910.

Hansen, Harry, The Chicago, Farrar and Rhinehart, New York, N.Y., 1942.

Kinzie, Juliette Augusta, Wau Bun, the Early Days of the Continent, Caxton Club, Chicago, 1901.

Mason, J., "Early Visitors to Chicago," New England Magazine, vol. VI, pp. 205–6.

Pierce, Bessie Louise, The History of Chicago, Volume I, Beginnings of a City, 1673 to 1844, Little, Chronicle Co., Chicago, Ill., 1914.

Quaife, Milo Milton, *Chicago, 1653 to 1835*, Little, Chronicle Co., Chicago, Ill., 1914.

Quaife, Milo Milton, *The Story of Chicago*, 1674–1910, Little, Chronicle Co., Chicago, Ill., 1916.

Index

173

175

Lawrence Cortesi

Lawrence Cortesi has been interested in writing since his high school days. His literary recognition came when he wrote and produced a one-act play for a high school assembly. The urge to write continued through service as an air force gunner in the Pacific during World War II and through a college career at Siena College, where he majored in English and journalism. After graduation, he worked as a newspaper reporter and then as an insurance claims investigator. For the past dozen years, however, he has combined a teaching and free lance writing career.

Mr. Cortesi has traveled through many parts of the country, especially in the northeastern United States to obtain background information for many of his writings. His first published book was *Mission Incredible*, which was followed by *Battle of the Bismarck Sea*.

His *Jim Beckwourth* as well as *Jean duSable* book are geared for senior high school readers.

He lives in suburban Colonie, just north of Albany, New York, with his wife (the former Frances Barringer of Glens Falls, New York) and five children. He does considerable traveling through the Adirondack mountains during the warm months. He enjoys bowling, swimming, and fishing and his principal hobby is model railroading. He runs a busy three pike HO line in his basement.